**Prepared by the
Department of the
Environment
and the
Central Office of Information**

© Crown copyright 1972
First published 1969
Second Edition 1972
Sixth impression 1976

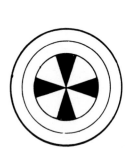

The Department of the Environment Manual

DRIVING

London: Her Majesty's Stationery Office 1972

Foreword

Somewhere among our millions of motorists there may be the perfect driver. It's possible. But unlikely. However long we have been driving, however experienced we may be, there is always something to learn. People who really take pride in their driving know this. It's one of the qualities of a good, safe driver that he recognises his own limitations. If safety is an attitude of mind, then humility is one of its main ingredients.

This manual is designed for all those who take their driving seriously. It is based on the Department's unique experience over more than thirty years of analysing, in detail, the everyday driving of millions of motorists. It answers many queries about points of technique or procedure which flood into the Department. It gives authoritative guidance.

Of course, good driving habits should be learned from the start. So the manual begins with learning to drive. But it isn't just an ABC for newcomers. Far from it. It has something to offer for every motorist, however experienced—and for instructors, too.

Anyone who has passed the driving test has shown that he knows the ingredients of safe driving. But all too often drivers let these standards drop in their everyday driving. This manual shows how they can keep the standards up—and improve them. It is an essential reference book for everyone with a genuine interest in driving.

Every year another million drivers take to the roads for the first time. Heavier traffic, more powerful and sophisticated cars, make good, safe driving more important than ever before. Higher driving standards are in all our interests. They make motoring not only safer but more enjoyable. Just reading *Driving* can't make a good driver. But it does point the way.

Acknowledgments

The Department of the Environment
extends grateful thanks to the
following organisations for their
help in supplying vehicles and
equipment used in illustrations
to this manual:

British Leyland Motor
Corporation Limited

Ford Motor Company Limited

Chrysler United Kingdom

Vauxhall Motors Limited

Contents

1 The good driver

With the coming of the 'horseless carriage' at the end of the last century, a new era in personal transport was born. The early motorist certainly had his problems—perhaps the biggest one being whether his vehicle would start and then continue to go.

This problem has almost disappeared today, but others have taken its place. More traffic and faster vehicles mean that, however safe and reliable a car may be, its driver has to have much more driving skill than ever before. Today's drivers cannot escape their own direct and personal responsibility for the accidents that happen on the road every year.

What makes a good driver?

A good driver has many things in his make-up. Some of these, such as experience and skill, will come only in time. But others —just as important—must be part of him from the start. These qualities are a sense of responsibility for the safety of others, a determination to concentrate on the job of driving, patience and courtesy. Together, these become what is generally known as a driver's 'attitude'.

Not everyone is patient by nature or gifted with good powers of concentration. But because attitude is so important a part of safe driving, every driver must make a real effort to develop these qualities—and this effort must start from the very beginning of his first driving lesson.

Getting into the right attitude will be harder for some people than others. It can be more difficult than the actual business of learning to make the car go or stop. All the things which go to make up attitude are just as necessary for the experienced driver as for the learner. So, before we go any further, let us look at these qualities in a little more detail.

Responsibility

As a driver you must have a proper concern not only for your own safety and that of your passengers, but also for the safety of every other road user, including pedestrians. You can do this only if you pay close attention to the varying traffic situations as they develop. Then you can plan your own actions well in advance so that they do not cause danger or inconvenience to others. At times you may be tempted to make a rash move—don't.

Concentration

With responsibility goes concentration on the job of driving. You must concentrate all the time if you are going to be able to deal with present-day traffic. Nowadays this is usually heavy and fast-moving and there are possible dangers all around you. If you let your mind wander, even for a moment, the risk of making a mistake is increased enormously. And mistakes can cause accidents. If you are tired, upset or unwell, or even thinking about something else, you will take longer to react. It is better not to drive at all in these circumstances, but if you have to, make special allowances for them.

Anticipation

Concentration helps you to 'anticipate'. In motoring, anticipation means acting promptly to fit in with what other road users are doing, as well as being able and ready to alter your own course or behaviour as a situation develops.

To those who do not drive, this quality of anticipation has the appearance of being automatic—and this is what it should become. Experience and anticipation together will enable you to act to prevent possible danger from becoming actual danger.

Patience

It is very easy to get impatient, or lose your temper, when other drivers do something wrong, or you are caught up in a traffic jam. But if you do, you are well on the way to having an accident. Never drive in a spirit of retaliation or competition. If the incompetence or bad manners of another road user cause you inconvenience, don't let your annoyance, even if justifiable, override your good sense and judgment. Attempts to 'teach him a lesson' don't do any good: there is no better lesson than a good example.

Confidence

The degree of confidence a driver has in handling his vehicle is, in a sense, part of his attitude to driving. New drivers will, of course, be unsure of themselves. Confidence grows with experience. But a good driver never lets himself get over-confident. This leads to carelessness, risks and, eventually, accidents.

Planned tuition

All the things we have talked about so far—becoming a safe driver by developing a sense of responsibility, concentration, anticipation, patience and confidence—will depend very much on getting good instruction from the start. Drivers often begin to learn with a parent, relative or friend and this allows them to get lots of practice at low cost. But although some non-professional teachers can put over the details of car control and road procedure within a reasonable time, many good drivers are not good instructors. They can ruin a pupil's confidence by leading him into situations he is not ready for. In other words, they often teach him to run before he can walk. And, of course, not all parents, relatives and friends are good drivers anyway.

A planned approach is essential when teaching someone to drive. Ideally, each lesson should be phased to suit the pupil's development. There are no short cuts to being a good driver, either in time or money. There is no doubt that the best way to learn to drive properly is to have good professional tuition—and plenty of it. It will prove well worth while in the long run. But you need plenty of practice too.

Mechanical knowledge

So far we have said nothing about mechanical knowledge—how a car works. It is not necessary to know all the complicated details of car construction to be a good driver. But the more you do know the better, because if you know how the different parts of a car work, and what happens when you use the controls, you will develop a sense of car sympathy. This will not only make you a better driver, but add to your interest in driving. It will also prolong the life of your car. There are a number of very useful books which explain simply how a car works. It would repay you to get one of these and study it.

The new driver will learn to use the controls more quickly if he understands how they work. In the next chapter we give, in simple terms, a description of the foot and hand controls.

2 Introduction to the controls of a motor car

The main controls of a car can be conveniently grouped according to whether you use your feet or your hands to work them. The *foot* controls, reading from right to left, are: accelerator, brake, clutch.

The *hand* controls are: steering wheel, handbrake, gear lever.

(If you intend to drive a car with automatic or semi-automatic transmission you should see also Chapter 16.)

Learners will be told about the controls by their instructors, but here we shall look at each control in some detail because, simple though they may seem, each needs a particular skill. Proper understanding and use of the controls are 'musts' for safe driving. Every new driver must learn these skills thoroughly—however long it takes. Here again, the experience and knowledge of a good professional instructor are invaluable, if not essential.

Opposite, upper
RIGHT—This driver has adjusted the seat so that she can reach the controls easily and comfortably.

Opposite, lower
WRONG—This driver is seated too far back from the controls.

The driving position

Before you can begin to work the controls properly you must be able to reach them easily and comfortably. Always make sure that the driving seat is in the right position for you. You should be able to push the brake and clutch pedals right down without moving your body forward. At the same time you should be able to hold the steering wheel rim, lightly but firmly, with your hands at or between the positions corresponding to ten minutes to two, or a quarter to three on a clock face. Your body should be resting firmly against the back of the seat. You can check whether you have got the right position by pushing down any two of the pedals: your legs should be slightly bent at the knees—not stretched right out.

As to height, you must be able to see straight ahead without having to peer over the top of the steering wheel. If you are very short you may need a secure cushion to raise or support you —unless you have a car in which the height and slope of the driving seat can be adjusted.

Seeing properly to the rear through the driving mirror is another 'must'. But we shall deal with that more fully in the next chapter.

The foot controls

Accelerator

The accelerator (or gas pedal, as some instructors call it) is worked by the right foot. It is linked to the carburettor, a device supplying the correct mixture of air and petrol on which the engine runs. The accelerator controls the *rate* at which this mixture flows into the engine, and therefore the power output of the engine. The further the pedal is pressed down, the greater the power output and the faster the car goes. When you let the pedal up, or take your foot off altogether, the opposite happens and the car begins to slow down (unless you are going down a slope). This is because the engine is trying to run more slowly and is acting as a brake.

The accelerator pedal is very sensitive and new drivers usually find it difficult to get just the right amount of pressure on it. Getting the 'feel' of the pedal needs practice, to avoid jerky starts or a roaring engine.

▇ Footbrake

The brake pedal, like the accelerator, is worked by the right foot. This is convenient, because in ordinary driving you don't need to use these two controls at the same time. The brake pedal is placed immediately to the left of the accelerator and should be worked with the ball of the foot.

Under normal driving conditions, this brake *only* should be used. (The other braking control, the handbrake, is dealt with later.) The harder the pedal is pushed down, the greater the braking effect and the more quickly the car will lose speed. In most situations only light pedal pressure is needed to brake safely and smoothly.

Training in using the brake pedal should include not only the application of the brake, but also practice in moving the right foot freely and accurately from the accelerator to the brake and back again without looking down at the pedals. This can be practised while sitting in the driving seat without the engine running.

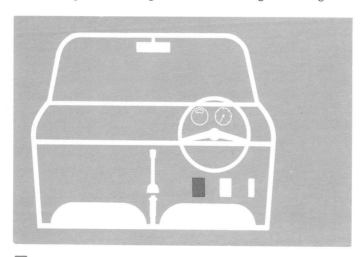

Clutch

The clutch is a device which allows the engine to run without driving the wheels. In its simplest form, it is made up of two plates. One of them turns all the time the engine is running; the other is linked to the wheels and is moved only when it is touching the first one.

When the clutch pedal is in its normal (up) position the plates are held firmly together by spring pressure so that the engine will drive the car. Pushing the pedal down separates the plates and breaks the link between engine and wheels.

To get a car on the move smoothly, the gap between these two plates has to be closed—but not too suddenly. This means letting the clutch pedal up until it reaches the point at which the two plates begin to come together. This point is called the 'biting point', 'point of contact' or 'take-up point'. With practice and experience, you will know just where it is. You will be able to feel it and also hear it, because the speed of the engine will drop.

Being able to sense this point is part of the secret of clutch control. The other part is being able to control the rest of the upward movement of the clutch pedal so that the two plates fit together without a jerk.

This needs lots of practice. You must be as careful to let the clutch pedal come up slowly as you are to use the accelerator gently. Ignoring these rules can cause a stalled engine or a jerky start.

The hand controls

 Steering wheel

This should be held lightly but firmly, with your hands at or between the ten-to-two or quarter-to-three positions. Always use both hands for the steering, except when you need one hand for another driving job. *Never* have both hands off the steering wheel at the same time. You will find that when the car is on the move it takes very little effort to turn the wheel. There is no need to grip it tightly.

The angle through which the front wheels can be turned is known as the 'lock'. The sharper the turn the more you will need to turn the steering wheel. When you turn it left or right as far as it will go you will be applying full left lock or full right lock.

The next rule to remember is not to cross your hands on the steering wheel when you are turning it. If you do you lose a lot of control over the steering, which can be dangerous. The correct way to steer round a corner is to feed the rim of the steering wheel through your hands with a pull-push movement. If you are turning left, the left hand should be moved to a higher position (but not past twelve o'clock) and the wheel pulled downwards, while the right hand is slid down the wheel. You can then push up with the right hand while the left hand, in turn, is slid up the wheel (see Fig. 1). If you are turning right the movements are reversed.

Where less steering lock is needed, hand movements may be shorter. For some changes of direction it may be enough to pull the wheel downwards and allow the rim to slide through the other hand.

As the turn is completed you must straighten up. To do this,

What the left hand does		What the right hand does
Slides up		
PULLS down		Slides down
Slides up		PUSHES up
PULLS down		Slides down

the steering wheel must be fed back through your hands in the opposite direction. We say 'fed back' because you must not let the wheel spin back on its own—there will be a tendency for it to do this. So keep control by *feeding the wheel back*.

❙ Handbrake

In this illustration the handbrake is shown between the two front seats. But it can be on the right of the driver's seat, or underneath the facia (dashboard).

The handbrake is provided to hold the vehicle still when it is halted or parked. In most cars the handbrake operates *only on the two rear wheels*. This is why it should not be used to stop the car while it is moving, except in an emergency such as the failure of the footbrake. Applying brakes to the rear wheels only can cause a nasty skid.

The handbrake is fitted with a catch to lock it in the 'on' position. To apply the handbrake release the catch by pressing the button, or other fitment, on the end of the handbrake, pull it hard on, then release the button. The catch will now lock the brake in the 'on' position.

To release the handbrake, first pull it as if to apply it harder—this will release the catch more easily—then, still pressing the button, the handbrake can be moved to the 'off' position. (On some cars, twisting the brake handle takes the place of pressing a button.)

Fig. 1
Turning left (see text on pages 9 and 11)

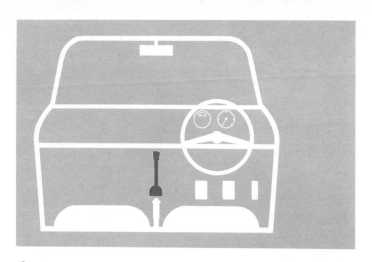

ⅼ Gear lever and gearbox

The actual position of the gear lever will vary from car to car, but it is usually on the floor of the car on the left-hand side of the driver or on the side of the steering column below the steering wheel.

The gear lever is used to change from one gear to another. The gears, contained in a gearbox, enable the driver to match the engine power to the speed of the car and the load it has to move. For example, more power is usually needed when starting off, to get the weight of the car moving, than to keep the car at a particular speed on a level road.

The number of forward gears will depend on the make and model of the car. There will also be a reverse gear to drive the car backwards. Fig. 2 shows some of the possible arrangements which are sometimes marked on top of the gear lever. The centre part, marked N in the diagram, is known as neutral. Whenever the gear lever is moved out of one of the gear positions and into or through neutral, the link between the engine and the wheels is broken even though the clutch pedal is not pushed down.

To select the gear you need, you first have to push the clutch pedal right down. Then you can move the gear lever into the right position for the gear you want. You will see from Fig. 2 that whenever you change from one gear to another you always move the gear lever through neutral. New drivers should make a point of learning all the gear lever positions so that they know exactly which way to move the lever without having to look down at it. With practice, changing gear will become second nature.

The lowest, or first, gear is the most powerful. But it will drive the car only at slow speeds, and is used for moving off, manoeuvring at slow speeds and climbing steep hills. After moving off you will have to use successively higher gears the greater the speed of

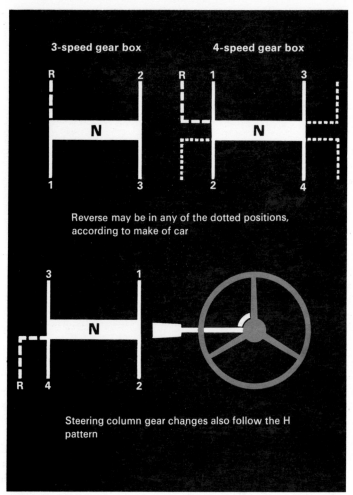

Fig. 2

Gear lever positions

the car—from first to second and so on until you get to top gear. This process is known as changing up. Top is the least powerful gear, but it gives the widest range of speeds. It is the third gear in a car having three forward gears, and the fourth in one with four. When you have to drive at a slower speed you should change to a lower gear. This is known as 'changing down'. We shall be referring to changing up and changing down a great deal—and explaining how to do it—in the following chapters.

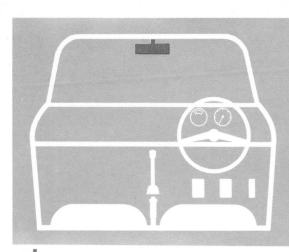

 Driving mirror

The most vital and important visual aid is the driving mirror. This is usually fitted inside the car near the top centre of the windscreen. It is so important that the whole of the next chapter is about how to use it properly.

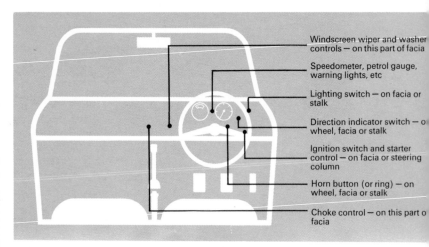

Windscreen wiper and washer controls — on this part of facia

Speedometer, petrol gauge, warning lights, etc

Lighting switch — on facia or stalk

Direction indicator switch — o wheel, facia or stalk

Ignition switch and starter control — on facia or steering column

Horn button (or ring) — on wheel, facia or stalk

Choke control — on this part o facia

Other controls

Visual aids

Most modern cars have dials and gauges on the facia below the windscreen. These tell you how the car is functioning. Apart from a speedometer and a petrol gauge, you may also have lights to warn you if something is wrong with the engine oil pressure or the electrical system; or to show that your headlights are on the main beam, or your direction indicators are switched on. Your instructor will tell you how to understand and act upon these visual aids.

Direction indicators

Most vehicles are fitted with direction indicators of the type that flash at both front and back (some have them at the sides as well), although a few have the semaphore type with a lighted arm. All indicators are worked by a switch, usually a small lever, fitted on or near the steering column.

Most direction indicators are self-cancelling, which means that as you straighten up after a turn the signal switches itself off. But be careful. If your change in direction is only slight the self-cancelling device may not work and you will have to switch off the indicators by hand. After you have made a turn, check that your indicators are switched off—otherwise you will mislead other drivers, possibly with serious results.

It is especially important to do this if your indicators are not of the self-cancelling type and have to be switched on *and off* by hand. Most cars have either a warning light or an audible warning (usually a ticking noise)—or both—to show when the indicators are flashing.

Windscreen wipers and washers

Windscreen wipers keep the windscreen clear of rain, snow or fog. They are worked by a switch on the facia or in some other position within easy reach of the driver. With practice you should be able to switch the wipers on or off without taking your eyes off the road.

When the road is wet your windscreen will collect dirt, water and mud. In these conditions a windscreen washer is almost as necessary as the wipers. It is operated by a switch or button, which squirts jets of clean water on to the windscreen. By using it with the wipers, any dirt on your windscreen can quickly be washed off.

Never switch on your wipers when the windscreen is dry. If you do you will scratch the glass because there are always tiny specks of grit on it. And a scratched windscreen can add to dazzle at night and in strong sunlight. So, washers before wipers—or before you start out, use a sponge and plenty of water to clean the screen before wiping it dry. You won't be able to see properly through a dirty windscreen.

In time all windscreens are likely to get covered with tiny scratches. Prevent such damage for as long as you can by keeping the windscreen (and windows) clean and make a habit of washing the wiper blades as well.

Lighting controls

Your car will have two white side lights, two red rear lights, two red reflectors, a white lamp to light the rear number plate, and headlights for driving at night. The light switch normally puts the side, rear and number plate lights on together, and then switches the headlights on as well. There will be two settings (usually operated by a separate switch) for the headlights—main beam, and 'dipped' for use when the main beam would dazzle. As we have already said, most cars have a warning light to show when the headlights are on main beam.

Horn

The button operating the horn is often in the middle of the steering wheel on top of the steering column. But it may be on the end of the direction indicator switch, or on some other fitting that can be reached without taking either hand off the rim of the steering wheel.

Ignition switch and starter

Every car has a switch, usually operated by a key. This switches on the electrical circuits necessary to start, and run, the engine. There is generally a red warning light which comes on as soon as the key is turned to show that the circuits are connected.

In some cars the starter is combined with the ignition switch and is worked by turning the key further in a clockwise direction. In others there is a separate knob, switch or button which has to be operated after the ignition has been switched on. It is important to release the starter as soon as the engine starts, and never to use it when the engine is running. Otherwise serious and expensive damage can result.

Choke

All cars have some form of choke, which is a device to help start the engine when cold. By pulling the knob out you get more petrol into the mixture of petrol and air which the engine uses. How far you need to pull it varies from car to car and depends on how cold the weather and engine are.

Always remember to push the choke in again as soon as the engine warms up. If you don't you will harm the engine and waste petrol. The engine will also run unevenly and too fast; this could be dangerous, and will certainly make driving more difficult.

Some cars have automatic choke devices which do away with the need for a separate choke control.

3

The driving mirror

The correct and frequent use of the driving mirror is so vital to good driving that the whole of this chapter is devoted to it.

How to adjust it

You must get the best possible view through the mirror. In most cars you will be able to adjust the mirror so that it reflects three, if not all four, sides of the rear window. You can then see anything that is framed by these lines. But in most saloon cars some parts of the bodywork will get in the way and cause blind spots (see Fig. 3).

These blind spots can be overcome by fitting mirrors outside the car, either on the front wings or on the windscreen pillars. When properly adjusted, these mirrors will help you to see the side areas which are not reflected in the inside mirror. Even then, there may still be some blind spots, so this chapter also describes how to allow for these.

To set the inside mirror correctly, sit in your normal driving position and move the mirror, holding it by the edges to avoid fingermarks, until you get the best possible view through the back window (especially to the offside) without moving your head.

Adjusting outside mirrors is not quite as simple, even if you can reach one of them from the driver's seat. But you must get them set properly. This is easier to do if you get somebody to help you. Many of them have a spring-loaded joint, so that they should flick back into position if they are knocked. But they sometimes remain displaced after a knock so it is always worth checking them before you get into your car.

Most inside mirrors are made of flat glass, and being close to the driver's eyes they give a clear picture of the road behind.

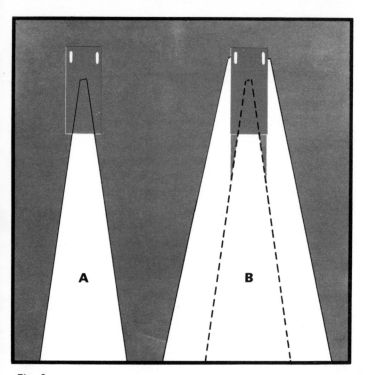

Fig. 3

How outside mirrors help to reduce blind spots

A   area seen with inside mirror only

B   area seen with inside *and* outside mirrors

Outside mirrors are usually made of curved (convex) glass, because they are farther from the eyes and this is the only way they can be made to cover a wider field of view.

It is more difficult to judge the position and speed of other vehicles when seen in a convex mirror, and you will need practice before you can do it accurately. You will learn more quickly if you make a habit of using the outside and inside mirrors together. Compare the different views they give of the same situation.

As an exercise, stop your car on the left of the road (choose somewhere sensible) and then watch the traffic approaching from behind through your mirrors. Try to pick out a slow-moving vehicle and then follow its progress until it passes you. As it gets closer, check what you see in the mirrors by looking round through the back window. Then compare what you see in the inside mirror with what you see in the outside one. The vehicle will seem smaller in the outside mirror than it does in the inside one. And because it looks smaller it will seem farther away than it really is. In other words, a vehicle seen in your outside mirror

A car seen in your outside mirror may be closer than you think.
In both these photographs the car is the same distance away, but it is
seen in a *convex* mirror (*above, top*) and a *flat* mirror (*above, lower*)

may be closer than you think. You can also practise this at suitable
times when you are actually driving, for instance, when you are
on a straight road and a vehicle is following at a steady distance.
But, of course, don't look round to check what you see!

How to use the mirror

The driving mirror is sometimes called the driver's third eye.
Even so, it is often sadly neglected. Just looking into the mirror
is no good. Proper USE of the mirror means looking in good time
and *acting sensibly on what you see.*

You must always use the mirror before signalling, changing
direction, overtaking, stopping normally, or opening your door.

Before moving off, make an extra check by looking round over your right shoulder

This is one of the few driving rules that are not subject to any exception or qualification. There are three very good reasons for this rule. First, if you look in the mirror you will know what is behind you, how close it is, what it is doing. And you will know whether it is safe for you to make a manœuvre. Second, you must know what is behind you so that you can judge when to make your move. Third, you will know whether you need to give a signal to help drivers behind you. (You may need to give one to drivers or pedestrians in front of you, but that is a point we deal with in Chapter 5.)

The fact that you use the mirror to find out what is behind you, and whether it is safe to make the move you want to, means that you must not leave it too late before you look in the mirror. It is just as important that your signal, which follows your use of the mirror, should not be left too late either. If it is late other drivers won't have time to act on it. So the first rule is: use your mirror in good time.

This leads to the second rule, which summarises a really essential part of good driving—the safe routine of *mirror— signal—manœuvre* (MSM). This means: *never signal without first using the mirror; and do both well before you act.* We shall be referring to this basic routine frequently in the course of this book.

There are two further points to be made about the mirror. We have talked about using the mirror before making any manœuvre, but a good driver should always know as much about the traffic behind him as in front of him. So get into the habit of frequent glances in the mirror, because a lot can happen in a short time.

Finally, it is even more difficult to judge the speed and distance of following vehicles when seen through your mirror at night. This needs a lot of practice. And you will also have to get used to the headlights of following vehicles being reflected in your mirror. If they dazzle you it is better to move your head slightly than to move your mirror—you may forget to readjust it.

Looking round

We have already mentioned that, whatever mirrors are fitted to your car, there will almost certainly be some blind spots behind (see Fig. 3). So, before moving off, you must always look round over your right shoulder, after using the mirror, to make quite sure that you haven't missed anything. Incidentally, other drivers who see you do this will know that you are waiting to move off.

Summary

1

All mirrors should be properly adjusted

2

Outside mirrors help to reduce blind spots

3

Learn to judge distance and speed of vehicles behind you, as seen in your driving mirrors

4

Always look in your mirror in good time before changing direction; and in good time to decide whether it is safe to make a move and if a signal is necessary. Remember the safe routine: *mirror—signal—manœuvre*

5

Use your mirror—frequent glances. You must know as much about what is behind you as in front of you

6

Before moving off, always make an extra check by looking round over your right shoulder

4

Beginning to drive: starting, changing gear and stopping

Every car user should get into the habit of making regular checks of the vehicle he drives.

Every day check:

engine oil

water in the radiator (if there is one)

that the windscreen and windows are clean

lights and indicators—to see that they are all in working order

Check, too, that your brakes are working properly as soon as you conveniently can after starting to use your car each day. And make a point of walking round your car at least once a day to check that there is nothing obviously wrong—a tyre going down, for example.

Every week at least check:

tyres—to see that they are at the right pressures (the car owner's handbook will give these)

battery—to make sure it is topped up

These checks are, of course, quite apart from the regular service checks that every car needs to keep it reliable and safe. Owners' handbooks show how often these are necessary for individual cars.

There is also a drill—rather like a simple form of 'cockpit drill' in aircraft—which you should use every time you get in your car. This is:

1 Are all the doors properly closed and locked?

2 Is your driving seat in the right position?

3 Are the mirrors clean and properly adjusted?

4 Have you, and your passengers, put on your seat belts?

5 Have you enough petrol?

Starting the engine

Having made these preliminary checks and settled yourself comfortably in the driving seat, you can now begin the drill for starting the engine (see Fig. 4):

1 Check that the handbrake is on by trying to pull it on further
2 Check that the gear lever is in neutral. If it is, it will feel slack and you will be able to move it quite easily and fully from side to side

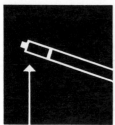
Handbrake on

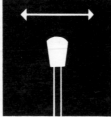
Gear lever in neutral

Choke if necessary

Ignition: switch on by turning key (to 1st position only in most cases). This also puts on the ignition warning light

Starter: turn key further; or use separate switch if fitted

Engine running: release key (or switch) immediately; use accelerator as necessary; return choke as soon as possible

Fig. 4
Engine-starting drill

3 Pull the choke out if necessary. (You will soon know whether you need 'choke' for your car and, if so, when and how much)

4 Switch on the ignition and check that the ignition light and oil warning light (if fitted) come on

5 Operate the starter

6 Release the starter key or knob as soon as the engine starts

On some cars it may be necessary to press the accelerator while operating the starter. On others this would upset the air and petrol mixture and make the engine difficult to start. Instructors will be able to tell learner drivers what is best for their particular cars.

If the engine does not start first time, don't keep the starter motor going. Release the key or knob, wait a few moments and then try again. When the engine starts, the accelerator may need pressing *slightly* to keep the engine running. But, as soon as it runs smoothly, take your foot off the accelerator so that the engine is running at its normal 'tick over' or 'idling' speed. If the choke has been used, push it right in again as soon as the engine is warm enough to run without it.

An important part of the starting drill is to check that the gear lever is in neutral. Hold the knob and not the stem, even when exerting sideways pressure

The red ignition warning light will usually glow while the engine is ticking over. If it does not glow, this may be because the engine is running too fast. (Have you remembered to push the choke back?) But the ignition light should go out almost as soon as the accelerator is pressed down. Check that it does. The oil pressure warning light (if fitted) should also go out when the engine is running. If either light stays on, switch the engine off and have the system checked.

Moving off from rest

When you are sitting properly in the driving seat and the engine is ticking over smoothly, you are ready to get the car moving:

1 Press the clutch pedal right down with your left foot, and hold it down

2 Move the gear lever from neutral into first gear. (If you can't get the lever into first gear, move it back into neutral,

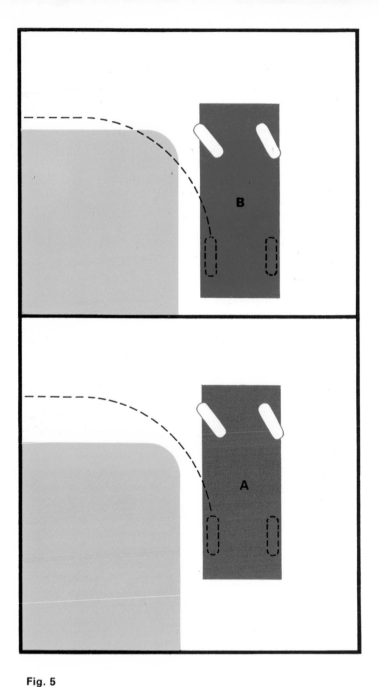

Fig. 5

You cannot steer your back wheels

and you must make allowance for this when turning corners. The back wheels will not follow the front ones, but will take a short cut along with the tail of the car, as shown in B. The correct position for turning a corner is shown at A

let the clutch pedal up, and then press it down again. Now try again to put the gear lever into first gear. You may need to do this more than once)

3 Press the accelerator down slightly with the right foot and hold it there, perfectly steady. ('A lively, even hum' describes the noise your engine should be making at this point)

4 Let the clutch pedal come up very slowly and smoothly until you hear a slight change in the engine noise. (This change in engine noise means that the clutch is at biting point—that is, the two clutch plates are touching—see page 8. With experience you will be able to 'feel' the biting point)

5 Hold the clutch pedal *quite still* in this position

6 Now make your final safety checks:
  (*a*) use your mirror
  (*b*) then look round over your right shoulder—take your time

7 Decide whether you need to give a signal to show that you are going to move off—ask yourself if there is any other road user (including pedestrians) anywhere near you who would be helped by a signal

8 If a signal is necessary, give it, either by direction indicator or by arm. (The signal shown in the Highway Code for moving out to the right)

9 When you are sure it is safe to move off, without getting in the way of anyone else (look round again if necessary), let the clutch pedal come up a *little* more—still slowly and smoothly. At the same time, release the handbrake—remember to put your hand back on the steering wheel straightaway. The car will begin to move

10 Press the accelerator further gradually down to speed the car up; and at the same time let the clutch pedal come right up—still smoothly—and then take your left foot off it

Getting these actions in the right order, and doing them smoothly and gently enough, are among the most difficult things a new driver has to learn. Don't hurry them. As with so much else, practice makes perfect. Once the knacks of holding the clutch pedal at biting point, and of not letting it up too fast, have been learnt the whole process of getting the car moving will soon become second nature. But you must get these right before you can make any further progress in learning to drive. Choose a quiet, level road for practising how to move off.

Steering

After learning the drill for starting the engine and moving off, it is as well to get some idea of the feel of the steering before going to the next stage.

The best way to do this is to find a quiet, straight road. Go through the drills for starting the engine and moving off, and then practise steering the car, at slow speed, in first gear. Learn to keep the car moving parallel to the kerb, and fairly close to it— about three feet away. Don't look at the front of your vehicle; look well ahead and avoid jerky movements of the steering wheel.

When you can steer a straight course with both hands on the steering wheel, try it with only one hand. Again, practise this until you can steer a straight course with either hand. As you take one hand off the wheel, stiffen your other arm slightly so that you do not pull the wheel down and swerve.

The reason for practising steering with one hand is *not* so that you can drive like this, but because there will be times—for example, when you are changing gear or giving signals—when you will have only one hand free for steering. And it is most important that at these times you don't let the car wander from side to side.

Stopping

Having learnt how to get the car moving—even if only slowly in first gear—you should next learn how to stop it. Although you will be on quiet roads with little traffic in the early stages of learning to drive, the drill for stopping (except in an emergency) is always the same. So it is as well to learn it thoroughly from the beginning.

You nearly always have to use the footbrake at some time during the process of stopping. How much pressure you need to put on the brake pedal will depend on how fast you are going and how quickly you need to stop. But there is one golden rule: never brake hard unless there is a real emergency.

You should always use the footbrake 'progressively'. This means that you should put a fairly light pressure on the brake pedal to start with, gradually increasing it as the brakes begin to act. Then, when the car has slowed enough, ease off the pressure so that it finally stops smoothly. There should be little or no brake pressure by the time the car actually stops. This is not only good and safe driving; it gives other drivers time to react, and prevents locked wheels and skidding; it also saves wear and tear on brakes, tyres and suspension.

Here is the drill for stopping:

1 Use the mirror

2 Decide whether you need to give an indicator or arm signal to show that you are going to stop

3 If a signal is necessary, give it

4 Take your right foot off the accelerator (the engine will begin to slow down and this will help to brake the car, as explained in Chapter 2, page 7)

5 Move your right foot on to the brake pedal and push it down, lightly at first and then gradually harder

6 Just before the car stops, press the clutch pedal right down

with the left foot. (This will disengage the engine from the driving wheels and prevent it from stalling.) Don't do this too soon, or you will lose the help of engine braking

7 Ease the pressure on the brake pedal as the car stops (unless you are on a slope)

8 When the car has stopped, apply the handbrake

9 Put the gear lever in neutral

10 Take both feet off the pedals

This is not a difficult drill, but like everything else it needs practice so that you can stop the car just where you want to. Pick out a particular point and see how near to it you can stop. It is better to find yourself stopping short than running past— you can always ease off the brakes and run forward a bit more. Pulling up at the kerb needs practice in steering too—both hands must be on the steering wheel.

In the next part of this chapter we shall be talking about changing into higher gears. Generally, you can stop the car without changing gear, although in some special situations, which we will discuss later, it may be necessary to change to a lower gear.

Changing gear

Having learnt how to get the car moving in first gear, and how to steer and stop it, you are ready to learn how to change up and change down—to which we referred briefly in Chapter 2.

As we said then, the purpose of the gears is to enable the driver to match the engine power to the speed of the car and the load it has to move. This is done by bringing different sizes of gear wheel into contact with the drive from the engine. And this, in turn, is done by moving the gear lever from one gear position to another.

Good gear changing depends on two things—knowing when to change, and knowing how to change. *When* is very much a matter of judgment and practice in matching the engine speed, by using the gears, to the work you are asking the engine to do. Until this judgment becomes second nature, as it will with experience, listening to the sound of the engine will help you to decide when you need to change gear.

There are no hard and fast rules about the speed at which you should change up from first to second gear; or down from third to second. This depends on the car you are driving and whether you are moving on the level, uphill or downhill. What we can say is that you should change up if you are going so fast that your engine begins to run too fast; and down if you are going so slowly that the engine begins to labour. Learners will, of course, be guided in this—as in all other matters—by their instructors. Guidance about the range of speeds for which the various gears on a car are designed will also be found in the owner's handbook— study this if you possibly can.

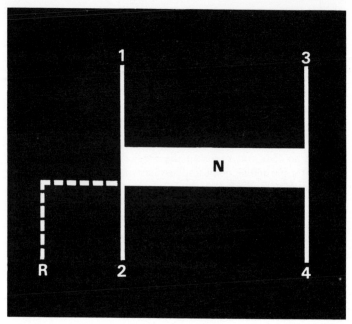

Fig. 6
A typical arrangement of gear positions

Now for *how* to change gear. First of all, as we said in Chapter 2, you need to know the various positions of the gear lever in your car without having to look down. Fig. 6 shows a typical arrangement of the gear positions in a car with four forward gears. Notice again the neutral area in the middle.

We have already been through the drill for getting into first gear and starting off. As your car begins to go faster, you need to change up through the gears, one by one. The drill is the same, whether you are changing from first gear to second, second to third, or third to fourth. Here it is, assuming that the gear lever is to the left of the driver:

Changing up

1 Left hand on the gear lever
2 Press clutch pedal right down with the left foot and at the same time let the accelerator pedal come right up (but don't take your foot off it)
3 Move the gear lever to the next highest gear position
4 Let the clutch pedal come up smoothly, and press the accelerator gradually. At the same time, put your left hand back on the steering wheel

The reason for releasing the accelerator at stage 2 is to let the engine speed drop, because it needs to be lower to match the higher gear, and so give you a smooth gear change. Timing the movement of the gear lever, so that when the clutch pedal comes up the engine speed is just right for the new gear, is a matter of judgment which comes with experience. Once again, there are no hard and fast rules, but your judgment can be helped by listening to the sound of the engine at different road speeds.

The drill for changing down is very much the same. The main difference is that you need to raise the engine speed to get a smooth change instead of letting it drop. In detail the drill is:

Changing down

1 Left hand on the gear lever
2 Press clutch pedal right down with left foot, at the same time keeping some pressure on the accelerator pedal
3 Move the gear lever to the next lowest gear position
4 Let the clutch pedal come up smoothly, and press down a little more on the accelerator pedal. At the same time, put your left hand back on the steering wheel

How much pressure you will need to keep on the accelerator pedal at stage 2, and how much extra you will need at stage 4, will depend on the speed of the car and on how fast you need the engine to run to match this speed at the time you let the clutch pedal come up. Again, the sound of the engine will help you to judge this.

Once you get used to it, changing gear is quite a simple process. Nowadays nearly all cars have 'synchromesh' on all or most of the forward gears. This is a device which matches (synchronises) the speed of the gear wheels so that the teeth of the wheels are moving at the same speed when they mesh together. Although this means that it is easy enough to get the gear lever into the position you want, there are one or two points you should always remember about changing gear.

Never rush gear changing. Smooth, even movements are best. Never force the gear lever. It will need some pressure on the pull or push when you are moving it, because you are disengaging one pair of gear wheels (as you move from one gear position to the neutral position) and then working the synchromesh (as you move from neutral into the new gear position). But you will soon get used to this. Remember, smooth and even. This calls for a light but firm touch.

You will notice from the diagram of the gear lever positions that changing from first to second gear means moving the gear lever backwards in a straight line. It is a good idea to put a little pressure to the left on the gear lever as you pull it back, to make quite sure that it does not slip to the right (into fourth gear) as it goes through neutral. Similarly, when changing from third to fourth gear, a slight pressure to the right will prevent the gear lever from going across neutral into second gear. There is the same need for this slight sideways pressure on the gear lever when changing down from fourth to third, or from second to first.

Lastly—practise. Learner drivers can get to know the various gear lever positions and practise changing them when the car is standing still with the engine switched off. Sometimes the gear lever will not move freely from one position to another without the engine running. If this happens, leave it alone. A gear lever should never be *forced* into position.

Moving off at an angle

When your instructor is sure that you can move away safely and smoothly straight ahead, you next need to know how to move off at an angle from behind a parked vehicle. With kerbside spaces becoming scarcer every day, and vehicles parking closer, this is something that all drivers must know how to do.

The drill is the same as for moving off straight ahead, up to the stage where you are holding the clutch pedal at biting point (stage 5 of 'Moving off from rest', page 27). Then you go on to your safety checks. But you have to add another one: 'At what angle shall I have to move out, and how far will this take me out into the road?' The answer to these questions will depend on how close you are to the parked vehicle, and how wide it is. The fact that you will have to turn out into the road means that you will have to pay even more attention to other traffic—both from behind and coming towards you. But the last question is still the same: 'Will I get in anyone's way if I move now—and do I need to give a signal?'

When you are sure that it is safe to go, you can get the car on the move using the drill described in 9 and 10 on page 27. But at the same time you have to turn the steering wheel enough to clear the vehicle in front. Don't forget to allow for someone opening a door of that vehicle. Move out slowly, and straighten up as soon as you are clear of the vehicle in front. In particular, be ready to brake—a pedestrian may come out from in front of the parked vehicle.

Moving off uphill

When you can move off smoothly and safely on a level road, either straight ahead or at an angle, the next stage is to learn how to move off up a hill. The tendency will be for the car to roll backwards down the hill, and the steeper the hill the greater this tendency will be. To avoid rolling back, you must be able to use the accelerator, clutch and handbrake together—and properly. Choose a quiet road where the slope is not too steep to practise this. Later, when you have got the idea pretty well, you can try it on steeper hills.

Much of the drill for moving off up a hill is the same as for moving off on the level. But here it is in detail:

1 Press the clutch pedal right down with your left foot and hold it down

2 Move the gear lever from neutral into first gear

3 Now press the accelerator down with the right foot—a little further than when starting on the level—and hold it there, perfectly steady. (You need to have the engine running faster because it will have to work harder to move the car uphill than on the level)

4 Let the clutch pedal come up very slowly and smoothly until the clutch is at biting point—when the engine note changes

5 Hold the clutch pedal *quite still* in this position

6 Now make your safety checks:

   (*a*) use your mirror

   (*b*) then look round over your right shoulder

7 Decide whether you need to give a signal to show you are going to move off

8 If a signal is necesssary, give it

9 Lift the handbrake and release the catch button. *At the same time* press the accelerator down a little more (how much more depends on the steepness of the hill) and let the clutch pedal come up a little more, very gently, until you feel and hear the engine trying to move the car forward

10 Then release the handbrake smoothly

11 As the car begins to move forward, press the accelerator down gradually to build up speed, and at the same time let the clutch pedal come right up, still smoothly

The most common faults are letting the car roll back—because the handbrake has been released too soon; stalling the engine—because the handbrake has been held on too long, or the clutch pedal has been allowed to come up too quickly or too far, or the accelerator pedal has not been held down far enough (or any combination of these).

Try to follow the drill we have set out without rushing it—and practise it until you have really mastered it. When you can start up on a hill smoothly and without rolling backwards, practise doing it from behind a parked vehicle—in other words, at an angle. This means combining the drill with the one on page 32 for 'Moving off at an angle'.

Other points about stopping

We have told you how to stop and suggested practising until you are able to pull your car up, without violent braking, just where you want to. But there are two more equally important points about braking—knowing your 'stopping distance' and knowing the proper way to stop in an emergency.

Knowing your stopping distance

The Highway Code says, 'Leave enough space between you and the vehicle in front so that you can pull up safely if it slows down or stops suddenly.' Although most drivers will agree with this advice, very few seem to put it into practice. This is probably because they don't realise how far they will travel before they *can* stop. It is a 'must' for safe driving to know your stopping distance—that is, the distance your car will travel from the moment you realise that you must brake to the moment the car stops.

Stopping distance depends on five things:

1 How fast you are going

2 Whether you are travelling on the level, uphill, or downhill

3 The weather and the state of the road

4 The condition of your brakes and tyres

5 Your ability as a driver

It can also be broken down into two parts—*thinking distance* and *braking distance*. *Thinking distance* depends on how quickly you react. Unless you are tired or unwell, the time it takes you to react will be fairly constant—well over half a second for most people. But the higher your speed the farther your car will go before you react. Even if you are going at only 20 mph, you will travel about 20 feet before your brakes even begin to act. At 30 mph you will go 30 feet; at 40 mph 40 feet, and so on.

Speed has even more effect on *braking distance*. At a speed of 20 mph your brakes, even if they are good, will take about 20 feet to stop your car on a dry road. If you are going at 40 mph (twice the speed) they will take about 80 feet (four times as far). And this is on top of the thinking distance.

Many people drive much too close to the vehicle in front, or too fast for the road and traffic conditions. This is probably because they think they can pull up in a shorter distance than they really can. And this in turn is often because they cannot judge distances properly. It is all very well to be able to recite a table of stopping distances, but it isn't much good if what you think is 120 feet is really 80 feet.

How good are *you* at judging distance? Try it out. When you are walking in the street, pick out something ahead of you—a parked car or lamp-post—and estimate how far away it is. Then pace it out—a good stride is about a yard—and see how close your estimate was. Even if you are spot on first time, try it again with different objects at different distances.

The real point here is that you should not only know what your stopping distance is at various speeds, but you must be able to judge pretty accurately just what this is in terms of length of road as you are driving. Then you must apply this in deciding how far you should be behind the vehicle in front.

Finally—a very important point. Braking depends above all on how well your tyres grip the road surface. If the road is wet or the road surface is loose, your tyres won't grip so well and your braking distance will be quite a lot longer than on a good dry road. We shall go into this question of braking in bad weather in more detail later on. In the meantime, remember to leave *much more* time and room for braking in bad weather.

Stopping in an emergency

A good and safe driver should never have to brake really hard, still less to make a 'crash stop'. But emergencies do sometimes arise—for instance, a child may run into the road in front of you— so you must know how to stop really quickly. (This, incidentally, is why the 'emergency stop' is included in the Department driving test.)

The main thing to remember is that although you must brake hard you should still follow the rule of progressive braking—that is, pushing the brake pedal harder as you slow down. Here are some other points about emergency braking:

Keep both hands on the steering wheel—you need the greatest possible control over steering

Avoid braking so hard that you lock any of the wheels— even if you don't skid sideways, a wheel sliding along the road is doing very little, if anything, to help stopping

Leave the clutch pedal alone until just before you stop; this will give some help to your braking, and usually to stability as well

Leave the handbrake alone—most handbrakes operate on the back wheels only, and if you put extra braking on them you stand more chance of locking them and skidding. (Of course, if your footbrake fails to work, you will have to use the handbrake)

If you are not moving on again straightaway after stopping, put the handbrake on and the gear lever in neutral, just as you would after a normal stop.

Many learner drivers tend to put too much pressure on the footbrake, and so lock the wheels. It certainly needs practice to get the right amount of brake pressure to stop the car without locking the wheels. But every driver should remember that the amount of brake pressure he can apply safely depends on the state of the road surface. If it is firm and dry, you can apply very firm pressure. If it is wet or loose, your tyres will have less grip and the wheels will lock more easily, so you cannot use as much pressure.

Finally, don't bother to give a signal if you are having to stop in an emergency. As we have said, you need both hands on the steering wheel. Nor need you make a special point of using the mirror before starting to brake. If you have been using the mirror properly, you should have a pretty good idea of what is behind you anyway. The most important thing, when you are faced with a real emergency, is to stop as quickly as you possibly can, with your car under full control.

Double declutching

You should be able to make a smooth change down into all your gears, including first. As we mentioned earlier, most cars have synchromesh on all or some of the forward gears. But if you don't have synchromesh on first gear, you have an extra problem in making a smooth change down into that gear because you have to do the matching of the gear wheel speeds yourself. You do this by 'double declutching'. Here is the drill:

1 Hand on the gear lever
2 Push the clutch pedal right down and at the same time let the accelerator pedal come right up
3 Move the gear lever to neutral and hold it there
4 Let the clutch pedal come up, press the accelerator pedal quickly and release it immediately
5 Push the clutch pedal right down and move the gear lever to the next lower gear position
6 Let the clutch pedal come up, at the same time pressing the accelerator pedal

The reason for engaging the clutch and using the accelerator at stage 4 is to speed up the gear wheel on the drive from the engine so that, when the gear is engaged at stage 5, the teeth on that gear wheel will be moving at the proper (higher) speed to engage smoothly with the teeth on the new gear wheel.

You will need to speed up the engine quickly by a sudden dab on the accelerator pedal at stage 4, rather than by a gradual pressure. How much you will need to speed up the engine will depend on how fast you are going. The higher your speed, the more you must speed up the engine. You will have to remember that the engine will begin to slow down while you are carrying out stage 5. So double declutching successfully depends very much on being able to make the various hand and foot movements reasonably quickly—a smooth rhythm is what is needed.

You can practise your first double declutching on a quiet, level road when going at a speed within the speed range of the gear into which you are going to change. Later, you can practise on slopes of increasing steepness.

Summary
1
The routine car checks: oil, water, clean windscreen and windows, tyres, lights and battery
2
The 'cockpit drill'; doors, driving seat, mirrors, seat belts, petrol

3

The drill for starting the engine

4

The drill for moving off straight ahead; and the safety checks—using mirror and looking round

5

The drill for stopping; progressive use of footbrake

6

Changing gear—up and down; the need for smooth, unhurried movements. Learning the right gear to use for different speeds

7

Moving off at an angle; the importance of proper steering

8

Moving off uphill; using the handbrake to avoid rolling backwards

9

The importance of knowing and judging stopping distances; and of not driving too close to the vehicle in front. Thinking distance and braking distance, and the effect of wet roads

10

Stopping in an emergency. How to avoid locking the wheels

11

Double declutching

5 On the road

Anticipation

In Chapter 1 we say, 'In motoring, anticipation means acting promptly to fit in with what other road users are doing, as well as being able and ready to alter your own course or behaviour as a situation develops.' Now is the time to see how anticipation should be applied on the road. One dictionary definition of 'anticipate' is 'realise beforehand: use in advance'. Anticipation in the motoring sense is simply *making early use of the available information.* In anticipation lies the answer to most of the questions a driver must always be asking himself—questions such as: 'What am I likely to find?' 'What is he going to do?' 'Should I slow down or speed up?' 'Ought I to stop—where exactly?' and so on.

In any traffic situation, there are some things that are obviously going to happen. A driver who uses anticipation can quickly make his mind up what these are. He can then pay more heed to the things that *might* happen. Of course, he needs to check all the time that what he thought would happen *is* happening. And because the traffic situation will always be changing, this process of checking and rechecking must go on all the time.

Take an example. On a clear, dry day a driver on a stretch of dual carriageway with moving vehicles in both lanes will know that the cars around him are likely to continue on their way at about their present speed. He knows a great deal about what is happening, and what is likely to happen, around him. He can therefore concentrate on other things, such as how far to the next junction and the unexpected event for which any driver should always be ready.

Compare this with the situation of a driver on a cross-country journey who is using a dual carriageway (which happens to be

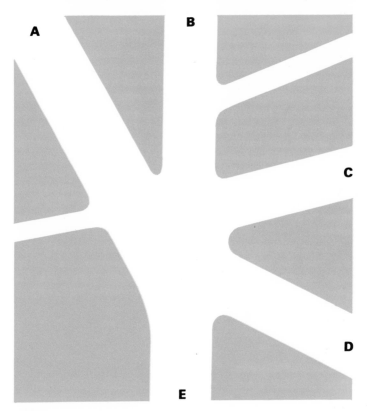

Fig. 7

There are many urban junctions like this one

the by-pass to a small town). The route is strange to him; it is about a quarter to six on a wet weekday evening and it is getting dark. There are all sorts of vehicles on the road and a succession of roundabouts at each of which traffic is joining, leaving or crossing the by-pass.

This driver has a much more difficult job of anticipation because he cannot tell in advance what traffic and road situation he is going to meet. He may not even be sure of his route. If he is sensible he will be driving much more slowly than the driver in our first example because he needs more time to weigh things up.

A different kind of situation is illustrated in Fig. 7, where the junction lies just out of the centre of a country town and carries local traffic on all roads and through traffic on A—D. None of the roads is wide enough to take more than one vehicle in each direction.

A driver taking the simplest route from E to A can recognise the things likely to affect him reasonably easily. A driver going from A to E has a more difficult job, and drivers coming from B, C or D to A the most difficult of all.

What are the factors here which make the job of anticipation more difficult for some drivers than for others? First, the *direction from which other vehicles approach*. A car coming from A, for example, will not ordinarily affect a driver going from E to A, whereas one from C will. But if the driver from E can see C's right-turn indicator flashing he will have much more information.

The second factor lies in *what other drivers are doing*. If the driver from E can see that the one from C is not only signalling but *moving* in a particular direction, he knows more about his intentions. All this merely underlines the obvious fact that early and accurate information, conveyed by signals, lane selection, change of speed or other driving actions, makes good anticipation by other drivers possible because the two questions 'What is he going to do?' and 'What ought I to do about it?' are easier to answer.

This all adds up to the fact that a driver should not only pick out, from the traffic all around him, information that will or might affect his own actions, but he should also make it easy for other drivers to anticipate his own actions by making his intentions clear in good time.

The use of signals

There are basic signals a driver can and should give to help or warn other road users. Normally (but with one exception referred to later) these are given by direction indicators or brake lights, as shown in Fig. 8. A visual or audible warning system will tell you whether and when your direction indicators are working. But it is up to you to make sure that you have switched on the ones you intended to! Make sure, too, that indicator signals are cancelled when your movement has been completed.

If your vehicle is not fitted with direction indicators or brake lights, signals can be given by arm as shown in Fig. 8. When using arm signals, give them clearly and decisively, using the full length of the arm. There is one situation in which an arm signal should be used—when slowing down or stopping for pedestrians to use a zebra crossing. Not only is this a positive warning to following drivers, but it helps the pedestrian to realise what you are doing—he cannot see your brake lights.

The important thing about signals, whether given by indicator or arm, is that they must be given *in good time* and for long enough for you to be as sure as you can be that other road users have seen and recognised them. You must allow other road users to see your signal, realise what you are going to do, and take their own action. This sounds fairly simple. But it isn't quite as simple as it sounds. There are times when a signal given *too* soon may confuse rather than help—for instance, when you are going to turn off and there are several turnings very close together. The general rule is:

'Give signals in good time, but watch out for situations which call for special care in timing.'

Drivers are sometimes in doubt about two questions: 'Should indicator signals be confirmed by arm signals?' and 'Should arm signals be confirmed by indicators?' The short answer to both questions is: 'Never as a routine.' For most intended changes of direction, an indicator is better than an arm signal. Usually, it shows up well and can be seen more easily (especially at night) and given for longer. But, again, there may be exceptions. For example, imagine that you are going to turn off to the right, but just before you get to the turning you need to pull out to pass a stationary vehicle parked on the left. You will have given a right-turn indicator signal well before you pull out. But an arm signal as well, after you have cleared the parked vehicle, could help a following driver to realise that you are going to stay out towards the middle of the road for your right turn.

Much the same applies to the other related question: 'Should I give a slowing down signal by arm as well as an indicator signal to turn left or right?' The important signal here, and the only one necessary, is the right- or left-turn indicator signal. This itself tells anyone behind you what you are going to do—which will include slowing down to make the turn. You must, of course, give the signal in good time, but it can't help anyone if you spend some of this time giving a slowing down signal before you turn. Indeed, it may confuse a driver behind you. A slowing down signal before your direction signal might make him think you are going to stop on the left—although in fact your real intention is to turn right. And if he begins to act on such a misunderstanding, both you and he could be in trouble.

Before leaving the subject of direction indicators, a further word of warning about the importance of timing your signals. The left-turn signal can also mean 'I intend to stop on the left' (see Fig. 8). Be careful about using it for this purpose if there is a junction on the left and you are intending to stop *beyond* the junction. A driver waiting to come out from that junction might assume—though he should not—that you are going to turn left. It will usually be better not to use the indicators to indicate stopping until you are past the junction.

Another point about stopping—but this time concerned with giving signals early enough. Most drivers react quickly when they see the brake lights of the car in front come on. But brake lights do not light up until the brake pedal is pressed, and even then some downward movement of the pedal may be necessary before they come on. So there is always a time lag between the moment you decide to brake and the moment your brake lights tell a following driver that you are braking. So here is another good reason for beginning to brake in good time. Not only will you be able to reduce speed more gradually, but your brake lights will

Direction indicator signals

I intend to move out to the
right or turn right

I intend to move in to the
or turn left or stop on the

Arm signals

I intend to move out to the
right or turn right

I intend to m
left or turn le

The use of signals

Arm signals to pers

I want to go straight on

Fig. 8

Stop light signals

I am slowing down or stopping

to the

I intend to slow down or stop

This signal should be used when slowing
down or stopping at zebra crossings

ontrolling traffic

I want to turn left

I want to turn right

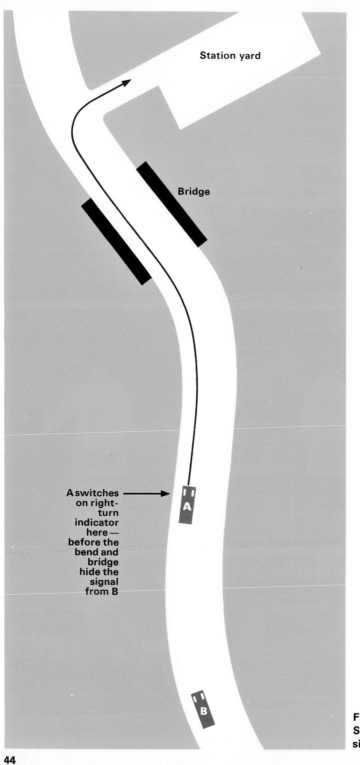

Station yard

Bridge

A switches
on right-
turn
indicator
here —
before the
bend and
bridge
hide the
signal
from B

A

B

Fig. 9
Sensible
signalling

come on earlier and so be more helpful to following drivers.

So far we have talked mainly about what signals to give and when. A point which sometimes bothers drivers is: 'Need I give a signal at all here?' It is sometimes said that if a driver positions his vehicle properly, everyone will know where he is going and what he is going to do; so no signals are necessary. But not every road user is another driver, and in any case positioning is only one of the indications of intention. Of course, if there are quite clearly no other vehicles anywhere near, and no pedestrians anywhere around, there is no need to give a signal. But if there is any doubt at all about whether a signal is necessary, it is better to be safe—give it.

Finally, remember that signals are not instructions to other road users. They are to tell them, in good time, what you intend to do. It is vital to use the correct signal and to make sure before signalling that what you intend to do is safe—by using your mirror first—*mirror—signal—manœuvre*.

Use of the horn

If you are driving properly and safely you will seldom need to use your horn. In fact, you should sound it only if you think that some other road user does not know your vehicle is there when he ought to. Remember that the legal description of the horn is 'the warning instrument'. On narrow, winding roads (which need great care anyway) the use of your horn will obviously help pedestrians or other drivers who cannot see or hear you coming. But don't use the horn instead of taking some other necessary driving action—slowing down, for example.

When you do use the horn, consider how long you will need to sound it. For pedestrians or cyclists whom you intend to overtake, a short note is usually enough. It is not too alarming. Longer emphatic notes are usually more suitable when another driver does not know your vehicle is approaching and there may be an accident if he is not warned.

Above all, remember that using the horn does not give you right of way. Nor does it relieve you of the responsibility to *drive* safely. Neither is it a safety valve to let off steam about the failings of other drivers.

There are certain legal restrictions on the use of the horn. You must not sound it while your vehicle is stationary, except to avoid danger, or in a built-up area between the hours of 11.30 pm and 7 am.

Headlamp flashing

The flashing of headlamps has the same meaning as the sounding of the horn, no more and no less. It lets other road users know that you are there. Headlamp flashing should not be used to give *instructions*, or to give information about your *intentions*. But it can be useful, especially on fast roads where there is a high noise level. Supposing, for instance, you are going to overtake and need to start the manœuvre from a considerable distance behind the vehicle in front. If you think that a warning is necessary, it is better to use your headlamps, even in daylight, than your horn which might not be heard.

The use of gears

The ability to change gear easily and smoothly is essential to good driving. Knowing when to change gear is just as important as knowing how to change, because to drive safely you need to use the right gear to match the particular traffic or road conditions. A lower gear gives greater control of the car in most situations. If you want to accelerate, you can do it more quickly in a lower gear. If you want to slow down, a lower gear gives a greater degree of engine braking.

Broadly speaking, the more powerful your engine the less frequently you will need to change gear. This does not mean that if you have a powerful car you do not need to use the gears, or that you have to change gear incessantly in a car with a small engine. Whatever car you drive, you must get to know how it performs and handles—uphill, downhill, round corners, loaded and unloaded. And this includes its performance in each of its various gears.

We shall be talking about automatic transmission in a later chapter. Here we shall deal with manual gear changes, in which the driver must always think for himself, weighing up the need for a change of gear and then making it. Get into the habit of thinking ahead about gears, which means sizing up the situation well in advance and knowing whether the gear you are in is going to be the right one for dealing with it. Sometimes, when overtaking for example, changing to a lower gear before you begin to pass will give the extra acceleration you may need in order to do it safely. Again, if you see that traffic ahead is likely to cause a check, change down in good time so that you can speed up more easily and smoothly as the situation clears.

The right gear to use will depend upon the situation you are in. The main thing is to make sure that the gear you use is the right one for the job. Driving in second gear and 'slipping the clutch' (holding the clutch pedal partly down) to keep the car moving, when you should really be in first gear, is bad driving.

When you increase speed, don't accelerate fiercely or for too long in the lower gears. This will only make a lot of annoying and unnecessary noise, and may harm your engine.

The clutch should always be let in (pedal up) as soon as possible after the gear lever has been moved into a new position. Driving with the clutch out (pedal down) is one kind of 'coasting'. This means that although the car is moving it is not being driven by the engine. (The other kind of coasting is to allow the car to run

When a car is driven round a bend or corner, extra weight is thrown on to the front wheel on the outside of the curve. This overloading is increased if the brakes are applied at the same time

with the gear lever in neutral.) Any form of coasting is wrong, because it lessens the driver's control of the car, particularly of steering and braking. Of course, technically a vehicle is coasting while a gear change is being made, or when the clutch is pushed down (out) just before stopping. This is unavoidable. The important thing is to keep unavoidable coasting down to the shortest possible distance.

Some drivers, especially learners, worry too much about losing speed while they are changing gear and therefore tend to rush their gear changing, instead of doing it deliberately. In fact, a vehicle will normally keep moving for a far longer distance than is necessary to change gear.

All drivers should be able to change readily into bottom gear, even if it has no synchromesh, without having to bring the car to a stop.

The use of brakes

Proper use of the brakes is another vital factor in good driving. Yet many drivers (even some who call themselves skilled) do not seem to know the principles of safe and controlled braking. Braking systems on modern cars are good and efficient, but however well brakes are maintained they are only as good as the drivers who use them. And even good brakes cannot do the impossible.

A moving car is in its most stable condition when it is being driven forward at a constant speed and in a straight line. When the brakes are applied the balance of weight shifts forward. This means that the front tyres grip the road more and the rear ones less. Because the front tyres are gripping more, the car gets more difficult to steer. This change in weight towards the front, plus the greater difficulty of steering, makes it unsafe to apply the brakes hard except when travelling on a straight course. The harder a car is braked, the greater the shift in weight. The faster the speed at which it is braked, the more difficult it is to keep the car under full control.

Hard braking while on a *curved* course, such as a bend or corner, will have even more serious results. The weight of the car, and a considerable proportion of its momentum as well, will be thrown outwards as well as forwards. The tyre on the front wheel which is towards the outside of the curve will be considerably overloaded and will be gripping the road surface much more than the other tyres (see photograph on page 47). This extra grip can act as a sort of anchor and make the car go into a severe skid. Such a skid can be so sudden and unexpected that the car gets out of control. Skidding will be discussed more fully in a later chapter, but we have mentioned it here because harsh and uncontrolled braking is one of the chief causes of skidding.

Ideally, any slowing down should be gradual and smooth, by making the brake pressure light at first and then increasing it. You can get very near this ideal by good anticipation, so that you give yourself time to spread your braking over *a good distance*. The difference in safety and peace of mind of all concerned (including passengers) between braking a car to a standstill from 20 mph in, say, 60 feet, and stopping it from the same speed in half that distance is obvious. But this is what progressive braking is all about—and there is a dividend of reduced wear and tear on brakes, tyres, and car suspension.

Gentle and progressive braking goes with early braking. Late and fierce braking is the sign of a bad driver. Of course, you must always be ready to brake very firmly if the unexpected happens, but if you anticipate properly the need will seldom arise. Never drive so fast, or so close to the vehicle in front, that you would need to use full braking to keep out of trouble. If the driver behind you is too close, it is a good idea to drop further back from the vehicle ahead. This will give you more space for braking and therefore reduce the chance of a bump from behind because the driver who is following will also have more time to stop. If you spread out a bit, he may even follow your example.

To use the brakes properly, you need to take into account:

1 Your own speed of reaction

2 The mechanical condition of your car—particularly the brakes, steering and suspension

3 The type of tyres fitted, their condition and pressures

4 The size and weight of your vehicle, and your load if any

5 The gradient of the road and whether it has a camber or bend

6 The weather and visibility

7 The road surface—whether it is rough, smooth, loose, wet, muddy, or covered with wet leaves, ice or snow

In other words, first know your car. Then, if you are driving with proper anticipation, and paying attention to the state of the surface of the road, you will have plenty of time and distance over which to spread your braking and so avoid skids. Prevention is better than cure. No system of skid control is so effective as driving in a way which keeps you out of skids.

Finally, a reminder about the brake pedal. When you take over a different car, get the feel of its brakes at the earliest opportunity.

The handbrake

Generally, when the vehicle is stationary the handbrake should be applied. When stopped at traffic lights or in a traffic block, for example, you should apply the handbrake and then put the gear lever in neutral. When it is clear that the wait will be very short (for instance, if you are in or behind a stream of traffic and the leading vehicles are beginning to move off) the use of the footbrake only may be safe and sufficient. But, as a general rule, you are safer with the handbrake on whenever your vehicle is stationary. However careful you are, a foot can slip off a pedal, especially if your shoes are wet. Or, if you are bumped from behind, your foot can be jarred off the brake pedal. (You may argue that if a moving vehicle runs into the back of another one which has stopped, the immediate effect will be less if the driver of the stationary vehicle has *not* applied the handbrake. This may be so, but what about the secondary effect? The vehicle that is hit would certainly be pushed further forward—much more violently, and possibly into another vehicle or a pedestrian.)

When you stop in a traffic stream, leave a good gap between your car and the one ahead, without undue waste of road space, of course. This will give you room to move forward a few extra feet if you see the driver behind coming up too fast to stop. It can certainly pay to keep an eye on the mirror while you are waiting to move off. When you are stopped on an uphill slope, there are other reasons for leaving a good gap. The car in front might run back before starting off.

The use of the handbrake when stationary is even more important in a car with automatic transmission. We shall look at the reasons for this in a later chapter.

Braking in general

To sum up, safe and controlled braking needs early appreciation of the traffic situation (anticipation), followed by gentle but firm and progressive application of the brakes so that you can spread your braking over the longest possible distance.

Learner drivers should regard the correct use of the brakes as one of the most important skills they will need to master. The fact that it is apparently so simple to press a pedal (or pull a lever) to make a vehicle slow down or stop tends to hide the fact that there are physical laws governing the momentum of a vehicle. As we have tried to show, the greatest safeguard for all drivers, new and experienced, lies in taking action in time and so 'spreading the load'.

Finally, remember that when you brake there will usually be other drivers who will be affected by your action. So apply the safe routine—*mirror—signal—manœuvre*. Always use your mirror before you brake (unless you are having to make an emergency stop) and consider whether a signal is necessary.

Driving ahead

On the road, as elsewhere, every picture tells a story. To be able to detect and interpret the vital clues in any driving situation, a driver needs to be alert and observant. Both these qualities call for continuous concentration, and no driver can be expert (which is another way of saying good and safe) unless he gives his driving undivided attention all the time. The good driver is constantly assessing the movement of *all* road users on the *whole* stretch of road on which he is travelling so that he can see things from an all-round point of view and is ready to react quickly and properly. The talkative man often becomes a silent one behind the wheel. This is simply because his mind is on his driving. But if you notice that the driver in front of you (or behind) is constantly talking and looking at his passenger—watch him. His mind cannot be entirely on his driving.

We have said before that good anticipation depends in the first place on early information. You get this by observing and judging the scene around you. As you drive, take in as much as possible of what you see in front, behind and to each side. Keep your eyes moving. Look well ahead and then near to you, and give frequent glances in the mirror. Keep a check from time to time on your warning and instrument lights. All this helps to make and keep you alert. Changing your field of view also helps to reduce eye strain.

Fig. 10 shows some of the areas over which a driver's eyes should constantly be moving, according to the traffic and conditions through which he is passing. No other vehicles are shown in the diagram but there are obvious places which a driver must watch. As he approaches junction 3, for instance, the middle distance view (C) will be very important. But he must still watch the immediate area (A) and have time to spare for his mirror view (B) to see whether any vehicles have turned out of the

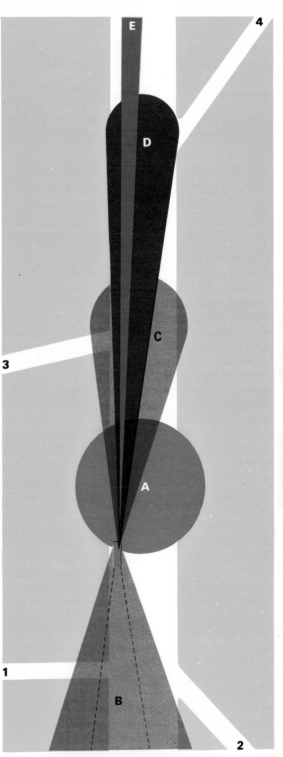

Fig. 10
The changing areas of a driver's vision

junctions (1 or 2) he has just passed. On top of this, he must take in view D to cover what is happening at junction 4, and also spare a glance for the long range view E. Truly, eyes everywhere! And the worse the weather, the more important—and the harder— these views are to pick out.

Here are some of the main things you should be looking for:

1 Other vehicles and pedestrians
2 Signals given by other drivers
3 Road signs and markings
4 The type and condition of the road surface
5 Movements by vehicles well ahead of you, as well as the one immediately in front
6 Side roads or hills ahead—the building line at the side of the road may show these

Keen observation can give you a lot of useful and varied information. The keener your search the better you will become at reading the road. The clues are there. It is up to you to find them, and use them. Especially in built-up areas, traffic conditions change rapidly and even the smallest detail is significant. Vehicles parked at the side of the road must be carefully watched. A driver who is apparently reading is unlikely to move off—but you cannot be sure that he or a passenger will not open a door suddenly. If someone runs out of a shop and gets into a waiting car, be ready for the driver to move quickly, perhaps without looking round. You may see only a puff of smoke from the exhaust, or the movement of his shoulder as he reaches for the gear lever. Small clues, but important ones which can be valuable to the observant driver. Keep a sharp eye on a driver who has stopped to set down a passenger. He may not use his mirror or look round before he moves off again.

All these pictures bring some message. Getting it properly and quickly often means the difference between a smooth reaction and 'panic measures'.

But however well you train yourself to observe, how much you see will depend on how *well* you can see—in other words, on your eyes. Ask yourself whether you can see as well today as you could, say, a year ago. Vision changes, and we tend not to notice a gradual worsening in our eyesight. It is sensible to have a regular checkup.

Some people have 'tunnel vision'. As the name implies, this means they can see only those objects which lie within a narrow field of vision directly ahead, and not those which lie to the left and right. To see objects in these areas they have to turn their heads, instead of just moving their eyes.

Your eyes are not your only source of information. Your ears can also warn you of what lies ahead. Everyone knows the warning of a fire engine or ambulance horn and bell. But how many drivers would take a factory siren or whistle as warning of a possible increase in traffic near the factory, especially cyclists? School hours, too, are a guide for the careful driver.

Reading the road thoroughly will give you plenty of time to plan, and prevent you from being caught unawares. It is an essential part of anticipation. And besides making your journey safer, it will also make it more interesting. This will help you to arrive relaxed—and in a good temper!

At first, new drivers will naturally be paying most attention to controlling their cars. But they should practise observation and teach themselves to read the road well. You don't have to be driving to practise this particular skill—you can do it as a passenger in a car or a bus.

Road positioning

Normally, you should drive well in to the left. This does not mean that you should drive in the gutter, but simply that you should not drive on the crown of the road. Just how far out from the side of the road you need to drive will depend on the road and the traffic on it. For instance, when driving in a town street where cars are parked at intervals along the kerb, weaving in and out between stationary cars is unnecessary and confusing to other drivers. It is therefore wrong.

Of course, we all have to 'get in' from time to time to help the flow of traffic. But, oncoming traffic and the width of the road permitting, you should normally drive in a line which keeps you clear of parked cars and leaves you room to deal with any of the dangers already mentioned—cars starting off, doors opening or children running out. It would be unsafe to drive very close to the kerb in a narrow street crowded with shoppers, many of whom will be walking or standing near the edge of the pavement. But if you can see in your mirror that the driver of a faster vehicle wants to overtake, and conditions permit, draw as far in to the left as you safely can and so give him as much room as possible.

The key to correct positioning is to be in the right position for the route you are going to take. You will then fit into the traffic flow and cause the least trouble to other road users. If you are turning left or going straight ahead, keep well to the left. If you are turning right, keep just left of the centre of the road.

The correct position for overtaking will depend on the circumstances at the time. This is one of the most dangerous manœuvres if it is not done properly. Always be very sure about what is involved and have things well worked out before going over the centre of the road. Remember that once you cross to the other half of the road you are on a possible collision course—in direct opposition to any approaching vehicle. (We shall be talking about overtaking in more detail in Chapter 11 and about some of the definite restrictions upon crossing centre or other lines marked on the road.)

The free flow of traffic depends very much on how accurately drivers position their vehicles. One thoughtless motorist can hold up streams of traffic. How often have you seen a lorry driver having to heave at his steering wheel just to get another six inches of clearance round somebody who could easily have stopped a yard further back or a foot to the right or left?

One-way streets

In one-way streets, position your vehicle according to whether you intend to turn left or right, or go straight on. If you are turning to the left, keep to the left of the carriageway. If you are turning right, keep to the right. If you are going straight on, be guided by the road markings. Where the road is not wide enough for a middle lane of traffic, you will have to choose the left or the right of the road. Having made your choice of lane, get into it as soon as you can, stay in it, but look out for other drivers who change lanes suddenly.

Traffic often moves very quickly in one-way streets, so keep your eyes skinned and watch out for vehicles overtaking you on each side. If you don't know the area in which you are travelling, you may reach your turn-off point before you expect it and not be able to get into the correct position for taking it without cutting across other drivers. If this happens, don't try a late dash. Drive on in accordance with your position and find another way back on to your route.

Lane discipline

Lane markings do two important things. They ensure that the available road space is used to the best possible advantage, and they guide traffic for the sake of safety. But they are no good for either purpose unless drivers keep to them. Keeping to the proper lane is absolutely vital in present-day driving.

Every road has lanes, whether marked or not. Where they are not marked (or where the markings are hidden), divide the carriageway into appropriate lanes in your mind's eye. Make it second nature to think in terms of lanes. Plan your course to avoid sudden changes and never move from one lane to another without good reason. Weaving in and out or straddling lanes or lane lines is bad driving. Once in your lane, stay in the *middle* of it until you *need* to move to another one.

Unless road signs or markings indicate otherwise, the drill is:

Driving along Keep to the left-hand lane where conditions allow you to do so. Don't use the right-hand one just because you are travelling fast.

Before changing lanes Check on the traffic behind (mirror) and signal your intentions in good time. If you find you are in the wrong lane, don't try a last-minute change—stay in it until you can get back on your route safely, even if it means going a bit out of your way.

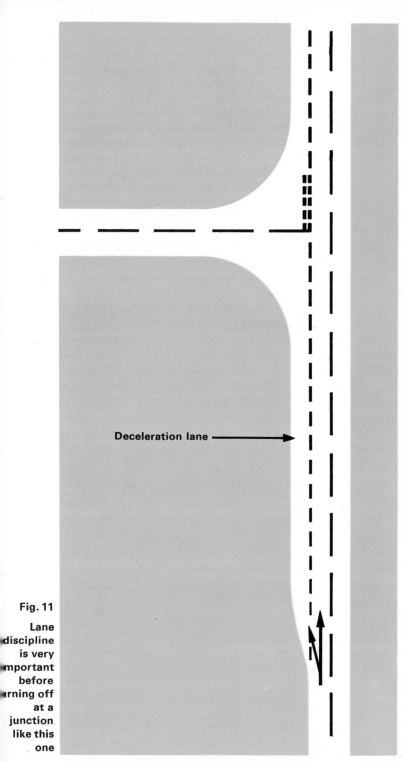

Deceleration lane

Fig. 11

Lane discipline is very important before turning off at a junction like this one

Approaching a road junction. Look out for road markings or direction signs which may tell you which lane to take. Normally, when intending to *turn left* from a road with *two* lanes in each direction, stay in the left-hand lane. *Going straight ahead* you should normally keep to the left-hand lane unless signs or markings tell you otherwise. Using the right-hand lane defeats its own object if drivers ahead are turning right. When intending to *turn right*, move to the right-hand lane in good time. If you are turning left, don't drive up in the right-hand lane to try to steal a march on other drivers who are correctly positioned on the left. Equally, do not use the left-hand lane when turning right. Trying to change back to the proper lane at or near the junction is a risky business.

On a road with *three* lanes in each direction, when intending to *turn left*, stay in the left-hand lane. *Going straight ahead*, take the left-hand lane (unless there are filter-left traffic signals), or the middle lane. When intending to *turn right*, use the right-hand lane. (We deal with the approach to roundabouts in Chapter 7.)

Some junctions have a deceleration lane which gives you room to slow down for a left-hand turn without holding up vehicles that are not turning left. An example is shown in Fig. 11. Watch out for these and get into the left-hand lane in good time so that you can turn off into the deceleration lane as soon as you reach it.

Remember that every driver is entirely responsible for his car being in the right position on the road. The practical message of this chapter is: 'Stick to the rules, then everyone knows what to expect.'

Summary

1

Anticipation—making continuous use of all that is happening on the road

2

Signals—when and how to use direction indicators and/or arm signals; the safe routine—*mirror—signal—manœuvre*

3

Using the horn—a warning instrument

4

Headlamp flashing—again a warning signal

5

Using the right gear for the job—dangers of coasting and slipping the clutch

6

Proper use of footbrake—the need for early and progressive braking; conditions to take into account

7

The handbrake—when to use it

8

Application of safe routine *mirror—signal—manœuvre* when braking

9

Reading the road, ahead and behind

10

Regular check on eyesight

11

Road positioning—keeping well to the left; one-way streets; the importance of lane discipline

12

Stick to the rules; then everyone knows what to expect

6

Approaching corners and junctions

Corners

Steering

The purpose of the steering wheel is obvious—to turn the front wheels so that the car follows a curved course instead of a straight one. It is equally obvious that the more you turn the steering wheel, the sharper the curve your car will follow.

If this is all so obvious, why have we mentioned it? To give us a chance to say that different cars steer differently—you may have heard the terms 'understeer' and 'oversteer'. A full description of the causes and effects of these differences would be out of place here. What is important is that you should get to know the feel of your car, and how it behaves, when cornering. Don't assume that all cars are alike in this respect. Remember, too, that different loads and speeds will also affect steering—and so will tyre pressures.

Acceleration

The dictionary defines 'acceleration' as 'making quicker' or 'increased speed of motion'. But the accelerator doesn't only speed up the engine when necessary; it also (as mentioned in Chapter 2 under 'Accelerator') does the equally important job of keeping the engine speed at the level you want. The right engine speed is particularly important when it comes to cornering. More important still is road speed—that is, the speed at which your car is moving. Your correct road speed at a corner will depend on how sharp the corner is, whether there is other traffic about, and so on. There cannot be any hard and fast rules about this. You will have to judge for yourself both the proper speed for taking each corner, and the gear which is low enough for that speed.

Some things are certain. First, that your road speed should be at its lowest at the moment you begin to turn the corner. From then on, your car should be 'under acceleration'. This does *not* mean —as the dictionary definition suggests—that you should be going faster as you turn. It means that you should use the accelerator so that the engine is doing just enough work to be driving the car round the corner. In other words, the engine should be just under load. The lower the gear you use the more control you will have just where you may need it most.

Another certainty is that using the accelerator too much on a corner is not only bad driving, but dangerous. It can make tyres lose their grip on the road and so cause a skid. So, 'not too little, not too much'. The important thing is to know just how your car will behave, and to realise that different cars handle differently.

There are, of course, many kinds of corners. The first, and in some ways the simplest, is where no roads join, but the road itself turns, more or less sharply. As we shall see shortly, you have to be in the correct position to take the bend, and also pay attention to the right speed, the proper gear, and—as described above—steering and acceleration.

The second sort of corner is where one or more roads meet, in other words, a road junction. The same principles of steering and acceleration apply here too, as well as observation, anticipation, the use of signals, gears and brakes, road positioning and lane discipline, as discussed in Chapter 5.

Bends

Before dealing with junctions, let us look at bends. This is where the road changes direction, but without the complication of other roads joining it. Some bends are so sharp that they might just as well be described as corners—and, of course, a bend could become a corner to a driver who approaches it too fast!

Left-hand bends

Keep well to the left. Your view will be restricted, so reduce speed. One question to ask yourself is: 'What will I do if the last vehicle to take it has broken down just round the bend out of sight?' Another thought is: 'Suppose someone coming the other way *is* being crazy enough to overtake!' You *can* increase your vision by approaching the bend from a position towards the centre of the road, but this may well tempt you to take the bend faster than is safe. You will also be closer to any approaching traffic and this means less safety margin—especially if someone is coming the other way too close to, or over, the centre line. Finally, unless very careful use is made of the mirror you may mislead or inconvenience following traffic. So, keep well in to the left, slowing down as necessary.

Right-hand bends

A position well to the left will give you the greatest field of view into a right-hand bend. But don't let this tempt or encourage you to enter the bend too fast. On some right-hand bends the camber may tend to tip you towards the left side of the road. This will make the bend harder to turn than you expect. It is too late to find this out when you are in the middle of a bend and your brakes can't help you.

Speed on bends

Your speed should be lowest as you start to take the bend. Then, with your car under acceleration (the engine just pulling), you will have stability and full control. Your passengers will also feel safer and more comfortable.

Junctions

For the rest of this chapter we shall be talking about approaching junctions—a much more complicated business than the corners and bends we have discussed so far, although the same principles of steering and acceleration apply.

Junctions take many forms. Most necessitate some change of direction, if only for proper positioning. The more complex the junction, the more changes of course or direction you will have to consider and, if necessary, make. For example, turning to the left at a junction will almost certainly be simpler than turning to the right; and the difference between turning right from a main road into a side road and turning left into the main road at the same junction can be tremendous.

The possible layout of junctions can vary from a simple T in a village street (*top left*) in Fig. 12 to a complex road system (Fig. 13). Between these two extremes lie a great variety of Y junctions or forks, neat four-square crossroads, roundabouts of varying sizes and shapes, and the staggered or offset junctions where drivers must feel their way (such as in Figs. 14 and 15)—not to mention flyovers and underpasses.

Advance information

As with any other traffic situation, the good driver finds out as much as he can about the junction before he actually reaches it. When you sight a junction ahead the first thing to do is to use your mirror. Then weigh up the kind of situation you are approaching. Note any signs (especially direction signs) and road markings. This will give you all the advance information about the junction, what sort it is, what traffic is behind you, and about the position and course you should take to go through it correctly and safely.

Application of safe routine (MSM)

Dealing with junctions is very largely a matter of turning corners or steering round bends. And even if you are going straight ahead

Fig. 12
Junctions
Some variations on a theme

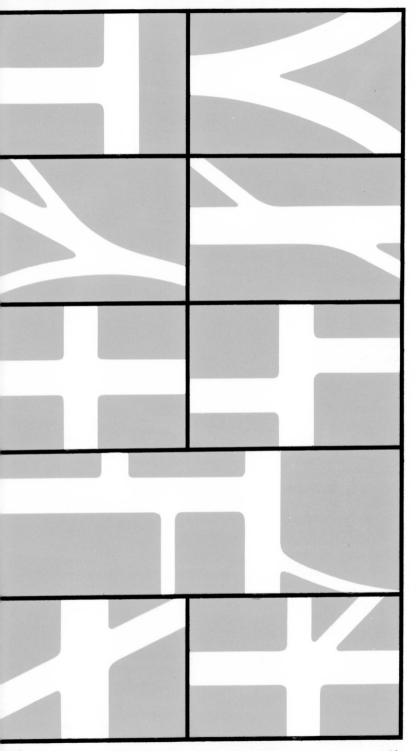

61

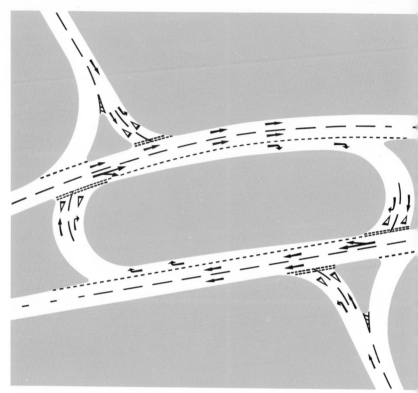

Fig. 13
A complex junction

with no need to do either, a junction is a hazard and you need to take the same precautions as you would for any other hazard. This is why the MSM routine (*mirror—signal—manœuvre*) should be used for all junctions, from whatever direction you are entering them. So, when you are sure what sort of junction it is and know what you need to do, use the *mirror* again, *signal* (if necessary) and follow with the *manœuvre* itself.

The junction routine (PSL)

We have just mentioned the MSM routine: there is another which must be applied when you move from one road to another through any sort of junction. It is PSL—*position—speed—look*. In detail, the drill when approaching a junction is:

1 Take up position
2 Adjust speed (by brakes and/or gears)
3 Look right, left, and right again *when you reach a point from which you can see* whether there is anything in the other roads—and stop if necessary

To sum up so far, when you see a junction ahead use your mirror and look well ahead. As you approach the junction apply the three steps of the safe routine MSM—*mirror—signal—manœuvre*.

Break down the manœuvre itself into the three steps of the junction routine PSL—*position—speed—look*.

You will then be able to enter the junction with all the information that early observation has given you about conditions behind you and the hazard ahead. You will be on the right course and moving at the proper speed. Then, at the junction, look right, left, and right again and decide whether it is proper to go on or to stop.

In the next chapter we shall be looking in more detail at what a driver has to do *at* a junction in order to enter his 'new' road safely. But before going on, we will look more closely at the things a driver has to look for and consider when approaching a junction or similar hazard, as well as having a closer look at how to use the PSL routine.

Assessing a junction

This means answering a number of questions about it. Here are some, not necessarily in order of importance, which have to be answered for almost any junction:

1 'What sort of junction is it—crossroads, T junction, roundabout, or some other arrangement of roads?'

2 'Do I need to change my position in order to deal with it?'

3 'Are there traffic signals?'

4 'Is there a STOP sign on my approach road, or on any of the other roads?'

Whenever you approach a junction it is necessary to ask yourself what sort of junction it is. In this case, the car coming from the left must give way to traffic on the other road

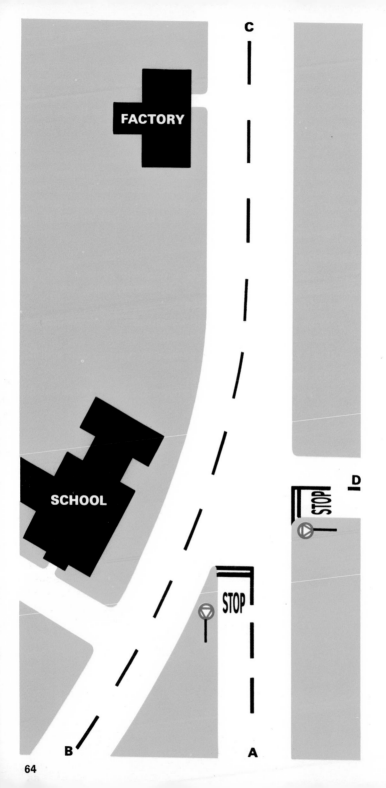

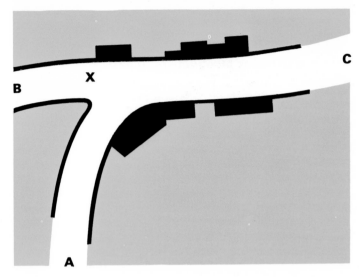

Fig. 15
High walls and buildings make for poor vision

5 'Is there a GIVE WAY sign? If not, where are the GIVE WAY lines?'

6 'Which seems to be the busiest road?'

7 'Is it obvious that I ought to stop anyway, or do I go forward until I *can* see whether or not to stop?'

Dealing with a crossroads can be quite complicated. All the junctions shown in Fig. 12, for example, are different, but nearly all of them might be regarded as crossroads by drivers who know them well. Yet, at many of them, a stranger will have to weigh up which is the main traffic stream and so 'feel his way' (see Fig. 14). And as we have seen, the main traffic stream may vary from day to day or even from hour to hour.

There are some junctions where you will be pretty sure that you should stop. Figure 15 shows such a junction—but the place at which you should stop to get a full enough view is not easy to find. A to C is the main road. There are high walls or buildings and no footways. If you are going from A to C you not only have to allow for the traffic from C to B, but also weigh up the risk from traffic going from B to C. Even with GIVE WAY lines at X, you still have to feel your way, because although any traffic coming from B should let you go first (and usually does) there

Fig. 14

An interesting junction Road A comes in on an up gradient while BC is the way to the coast. While this is a busy Y junction, school-children and factory workers use roads A and D. This means that there is often a crossroads in operation and two T junctions as well. Although there are STOP signs on A and D, this is very much a place where a driver must 'feel his way'

may always be the odd vehicle that doesn't. GIVE WAY lines may be hard to see in bad weather.

Application of the MSM/PSL routines

Let us see how you should use these routines at the junction shown in Fig. 15, when you are going from A to C. First, use the *mirror* and *signal* with the right-turn indicator. You will know who is behind, and following traffic will know that you are going to turn right along road C. Next, the *manœuvre* of making the right turn at the junction. *Position* is obviously critical in such a narrow and restricted place, and *speed* must drop until you are moving so slowly that you just roll forward to make the stop which is obviously necessary here for you to have time to *look* right, left, and right again. You must 'feel your way' so that, in order to see properly, you do not get so far forward on A that you are to some extent in the way of a driver going from C to B. Incidentally, a driver going from C to B must be ready to feel his way forward too.

Narrow corners like this limit your field of vision, and there are many such corners in the streets of older towns. But similar conditions can arise at any junction of narrow roads. And if large vehicles are turning or unloading, there is need for a high degree of careful driving and accurate judgment from drivers. Very careful choice of *position*, low *speed* and a readiness to stop, with a most careful choice of stopping position from which to *look* without blocking other drivers unnecessarily, are all called for in such places.

At more complex road junctions (such as the one illustrated in Fig. 13), you should use the mirror as soon as you see the sign that indicates your need to change lanes or position for your route. Then signal and, provided you can do so safely, change lanes.

You are now ready to weigh up the junction itself or, if it is a very complex one, the first part of it. At most junctions there will be signs and other markings which will enable you to decide on your proper course right through the junction—but give yourself room to see them by leaving a good gap between yourself and the vehicle in front.

More about the junction routine (PSL)

PSL—position

Generally speaking, the earlier you get your vehicle into position the easier it is to do so. Early positioning also helps other drivers to know what you are going to do. Late positioning hinders the flow of traffic and can be dangerous.

In some situations you may need to change *speed* at the same time as you are changing position. In others you may need to change *speed* in order to change *position*, and then to make a further change of speed. But position should be the first thing you think of when approaching and negotiating a junction.

PSL—speed

The process of adjusting *speed* on the approach to a junction can vary in a number of ways. You may need to use the brakes and/or gears in differing order and proportions according to the circumstances. On a more or less level road it may be enough to release the accelerator and wait for your speed to drop. On an uphill slope a change down may be necessary. Again, you may already be in the right gear; or you may need to change down to help you slow down. All this will depend on the amount of traffic, the size and layout of the junction, and whether there are gradients and how steep they are.

You may see the point at which your own road joins another so far ahead that an upward change of gear is necessary to make a reasonably brisk drive to that point. Slip roads and acceleration lanes are examples of this.

Apart from the adjustment of speed to carry you far enough forward at a junction, there is the important question of bringing your speed down low enough to have time to carry out the next step of the routine—looking.

PSL—look

Look right, left, and right again *when you reach a point from which you can see*—and stop if necessary. It may seem too obvious to mention that it is useless to look right and left before you can see what you are looking for. Yet, looking before they can see the whole junction is a mistake made not only by learner drivers. Many an experienced driver has to get himself out of a tight place he should never have got into. Did he look? Did he look before he could really see? Did he allow for the fact that the pedestrians coming along the pavement were blocking his view? Did his adjustment of speed give him *time to look*—and time to stop?

To summarise, we have now looked at several sorts of junctions, including those which call for particularly careful judgment of speed and position where space is limited. We have seen too that a driver may find himself in a large system of road junctions where he actually drives from manœuvre to manœuvre within the same system, changing lanes here, turning or stopping there, and so on. This represents one extreme; between this and the simplest junction lie a multitude of others. But the routine of MSM (*mirror—signal—manœuvre*), with the third step—*manœuvre*—broken down into PSL (*position—speed—look*) is common to them all. The final action of looking—from a position where he can actually see into the whole junction—is essential before a driver can be sure that he can safely turn into, or cross, the junction.

Summary

1

The importance of getting to know how your car behaves in steering round a corner

2

Judging the right gear and road speed at corners

3

Cornering 'under acceleration'—not too little, not too much

4

Keeping well to the left in both left-hand and right-hand bends

5

Speed at bends

6

Approaching a junction—the need for advance information; the particular importance of the *mirror—signal—manœuvre* and *position—speed—look* routines

7

Assessing a junction—the questions to ask yourself

8

More about the *mirror—signal—manœuvre* and *position—speed—look* routines

7

Emerging at junctions

At every junction, a driver leaves one road and turns into, crosses or joins another one. This is what is meant by 'emerging'. In Chapter 6 we showed how a driver should deal with a junction up to the point at which he must *look*, and stop if necessary. But what exactly should he look for, and how does what he sees enable him to decide whether to wait or go on?

The most obvious thing to look for is the approach of traffic —particularly from the right, which is the greater danger. The decision to stop is sometimes made for you by STOP signs or traffic signals, or by a policeman or traffic warden. At other places it may be obvious that you will have to wait for a gap in a stream of vehicles before you can join or cross a road. At other times GIVE WAY signs and/or lines will remind you of the particular need to judge the speed and course of other vehicles. GIVE WAY does not necessarily mean that you must come to a stop, especially where you can see into the major road clearly so that you can fit in safely. But you must let vehicles on the major road go first, and not *enter* the junction unless and until you can do so without getting in their way.

If you have stopped at a junction you then have to make a second decision: When is it safe to go on? This may mean looking again and again. Even when traffic is controlled by signals, the green light means only that you may go on if the way is clear. You must still take special care if you are turning left or right and, in particular, you should give way to pedestrians who are crossing (see also Chapter 12). The same applies to junctions controlled by a policeman or traffic warden when you get his signal to move.

At any junction, therefore, you have to decide *whether* to wait or go on. If you stop, you will then have to decide *when* to go on.

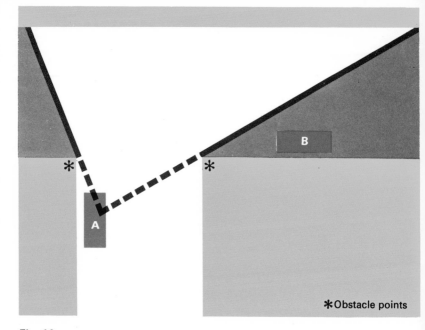

*Obstacle points

Fig. 16

Obstacle points and the driver's zone of vision
At every corner or junction there is some object or 'obstacle point'(*)
beyond which the driver cannot see. In the diagram above the
obstacle points are shown as the corners of buildings at a T junction,
but they could equally well be fences, hedges, trees, vehicles or
pedestrians. The zone of vision opens up as the driver approaches the
corner, but at the point A has reached, which is less than one car
length from the corner, he still can't see B coming

In all cases you need to have a full view. This brings us to the
important subject of 'zones of vision'.

Zones of vision

A driver's field of view enables him to see a stretch of the road in
front and behind him. His vision is normally limited only by
other vehicles or buildings, or by the framing and pillars of the
windscreen and windows of his vehicle. Sometimes his view can
also be impaired by weather conditions, making it necessary for
him to slow down or even stop.

Coming up to a junction is, in some ways, rather like running
into a patch of fog. Consider the extreme case of a driver
approaching a blind corner in a narrow street, with a lorry or bus
behind him. His field of view almost disappears. In front he can
see only a strip, a few feet wide, of the road he is to enter. Behind,
only a large radiator. This can occur on any road, however wide,
when a stream of traffic is approaching a junction. In fact, road

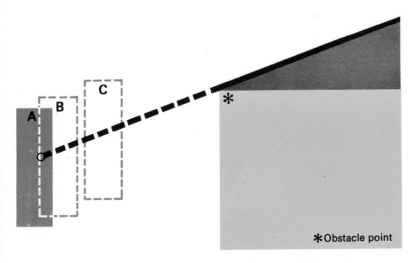

*Obstacle point

Fig. 17

The nearer an object is to your eyes, the more it blocks your view
In the diagram above it is interesting to note that from A the driver
gets a view to the right while his car is still behind the obstacle line.
If he had approached the junction in positions B or C he would have
to be further forward before getting the same view. At position C his
car is as far in front of the obstacle line as it is behind it at position A.
Always be on the look-out for obstacle points which limit your zone of
vision. They need checking even at that most familiar corner—the one
at the end of the road where you live

junctions are nearly always places where vision tends to be poor;
yet a good view into the other roads which make up a junction is
essential. This view into the other road or roads is called the
'zone of vision' (see Fig. 16).

Although the zone of vision gets wider as you get nearer the
junction, it is surprising—especially to learner drivers—how
close you must be before it widens enough for you to see far
enough into the other roads. Figs. 17 and 18 show why the last
few feet are so critical in giving you your zone of vision.

How far forward?

Once you have spotted the obstacle points and can begin to see
into the junction, you must decide how far forward to go. There
are two reasons for this. First, you must be far enough forward to
be able to *look*. Second, if you have to wait you must stop in a
safe position. So the answer to the question 'How far forward?' is:
With your eyes far enough forward to be able to look right, left, and

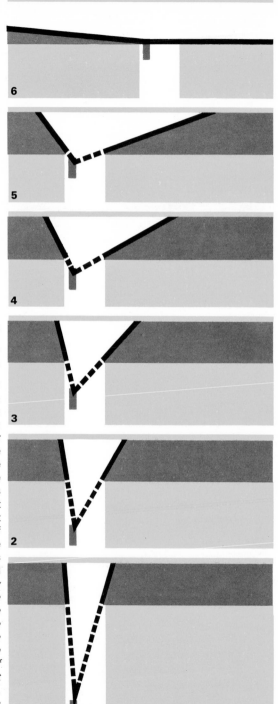

Fig. 18

Widening the zone of vision

Reading upwards from 1 to 5, each successive plan shows the car twice as close to the obstacle line. At 5 the car is 16 times closer than it was at 1, but the zone of vision into the major road has not increased very much. *Only when the driver's eyes are level with the obstacle line can he have a proper zone of vision so that he can look, and act, with confidence*

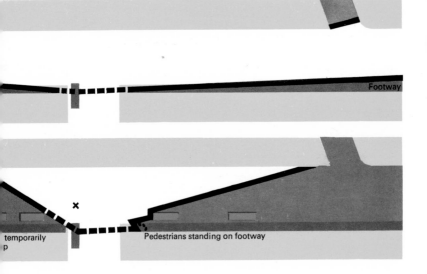

Fig. 19

How far forward?

Above: The driver's zone of vision is satisfactory when the front of his vehicle is level with the kerb-line and his eyes are on a line with the buildings to left and right. *Below:* The same junction but with quite different conditions. The delivery van parked at the kerbside and the two or three pedestrians standing on the pavement form a screen to the right of the driver, and stationary vehicles block his view to the left. To see enough the driver needs to move forward until his eyes are at point X

right again, so that you have a full view of the junction before deciding whether *to wait or go on*.

Fig. 18 shows such a position at 6. In the lower diagrams the zone of vision is shown widening as the car moves from positions 1 to 5. But even at 5 it is not wide enough. Notice that at position 6, where there is a proper zone of vision both ways, the driver's eyes are level with the right-hand obstacle point.

Notice that the reference is to 'eyes' and not to the front of the car. Obstacle points can vary from junction to junction. They can even vary at the same junction at different times, as is shown in Fig. 19.

Road width and the zone of vision

We saw in Fig. 17 that your distance from the right-hand obstacle point at a junction is important. Fig. 20 shows why careful positioning is so important, especially on a narrow road, and how little you can see until your eyes are level with the obstacle line. Then you have much the same view as you would have from a

Fig. 20 Zones of vision

The cars above are only one length from the obstacle line, but neither driver has more than a fraction of the zone of vision he needs in order to *look* properly

In the diagram below, with the cars a length further forward, the zone of vision is still too narrow for the drivers to be able to *look* properly

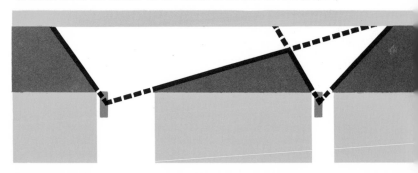

Now, with the drivers' eyes up to the line (*below*), they can see both ways and *look* to some purpose

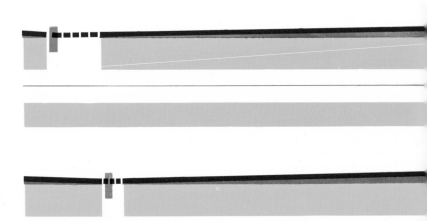

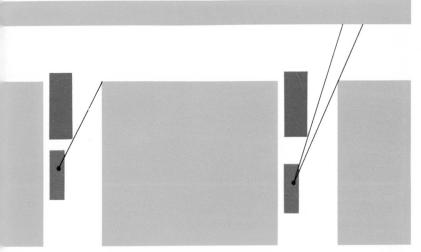

Fig. 21 The vehicle in front at junctions

This shows how your vision can be improved by careful positioning of your car. *Left:* In this position the following driver's zone of vision is completely blocked by the obstacle points. *Right:* From only a few feet further back, it is possible to see something of the road ahead, say, whether it is busy or whether it is a shopping street or bus route

wider road. Observation, anticipation, positioning—getting far enough forward to *look* without blocking other traffic—all have to be judged very carefully when emerging from a narrow road.

The vehicle ahead

So far we have considered the zone of vision only when the road ahead is clear. A bus or large vehicle in front of you can reduce your zone of vision to nothing at a narrow junction, as Fig. 21 illustrates.

We shall be looking at the question 'How far behind the vehicle ahead?' in greater detail later on. The point to remember here is that, whatever the situation, the closer you are to the vehicle in front the less you will be able to see. At junctions it may also mean that you do not notice direction and other road signs or markings in time to act on them.

Watching for other vehicles

It is not always easy to judge the speed and distance of an approaching vehicle, especially if it is coming straight towards you. It is a little easier if it is coming at an angle or on a curve, because you will probably be able to 'time it' as it passes lamp-posts, telegraph poles and so on. Remember, too, that if the

Fig. 22 Dead ground

Anything on the road between A and B is hidden from the driver of the red car. Overhanging branches can have the same effect on roads without dips

vehicle is coming downhill it may be travelling faster than you think. On the other hand, don't expect it to be crawling just because it is coming uphill.

Besides judging the speed and distance of vehicles you can see, don't forget that there may be other vehicles quite close that you can't see. Watch out for 'dead ground' where the road dips and a car can be hidden. An example of this is shown in Fig. 22. Look out, too, for overhanging branches which can hide a considerable stretch of straight road when they are leafy. Again, a car parked off the road, perhaps at an angle, can hide oncoming vehicles at a junction. This is really an obstacle point, but a car may come up and park while you are waiting at a junction, so be ready to re-assess your zone of vision and to move as necessary.

Keep a particular look-out for cyclists and motor-cyclists who may not be too easily seen.

Finally, remember that poor weather conditions can complicate the whole business of *looking* at a junction, however wide and full your zone of vision would otherwise be. So take particular care to *make sure* before going on.

Wait or go on?

It is only when you have got into a position from which you can see clearly both ways into a junction that you can answer the question: 'Wait or go on?' If there is a vehicle coming from the right which is very close, the answer is obvious—you stop and wait. It may be equally obvious that any approaching vehicles are so far off that you can go on with perfect safety for everyone concerned. Where, however, a vehicle is coming towards you at such a distance or at such a speed that you have the least doubt about being able to go safely in front of it, you should stop and wait.

To put it the other way round, you must be careful to join or cross the path of an oncoming vehicle *only* when it is far enough away to make it quite safe for you to do so. To force other drivers to change their plans is a dangerous business. This is very much our basic practical message: Stick to the rules and everybody concerned knows what to expect. At junctions, the rules really mean that you should be prepared to fit in safely with other traffic by adjusting your speed or position (or both) and, if that is not enough, you should stop and wait.

Timing your approach

Most of the examples given so far have dealt with zones of vision in rather narrow and closed-in situations. Now let us look at the situation of two drivers on the same stretch of road, whose problems in timing and observation are quite different.

Fig. 23 shows the approach to a T junction in open country where visibility is so good (because there are no obstacle points) that you can spread assessment of the junction by using the *mirror—signal—manœuvre* and the *position—speed—look* routines over a long stretch of road. You can do the PSL steps over and over again. A complete MSM and PSL routine is needed again for the minor junction with the narrow road, B. After this you can resume the PSL routine to negotiate the T junction itself. The significant thing about this situation is that, because there is good visibility, speeds will tend to be high and you therefore need to know all the time what is going on at, and near, the junctions.

But this situation is very different from that of the driver coming out of road B. Immediately after entering road A he must fit in the whole process of assessing the junction—*mirror—signal—position—speed—look*—in the short distance between the exit from road B and the junction with road CD.

The new driver at junctions

Before we leave the subject of looking (and waiting) at junctions, a special word to learner drivers. As a learner, you will be conscious of other drivers lining up behind you at junctions. Don't let the fact that you are first in the queue influence your judgment about when to go on. What *you* see when you look must decide your action, and nothing else. After all, the chap behind you has been a learner too.

On the 'new' road

Having decided that it is safe to emerge at the junction, you go forward on to your 'new' road. At once you will have another set of questions to answer, varying with the sort of road it is and the traffic on it. They will include:

1 'What is behind me now?' (mirror)
2 'Do I need to adjust my position?' (lane discipline)

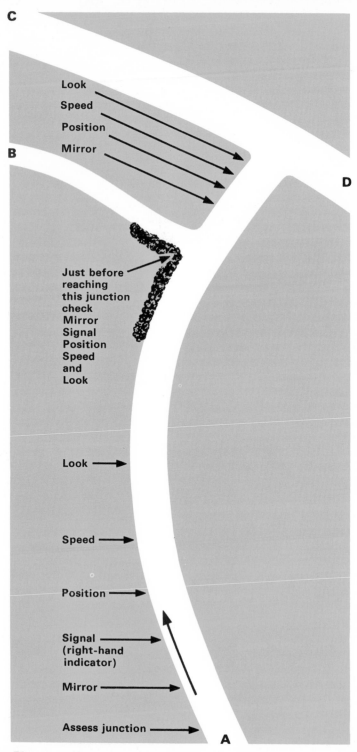

C

Look

Speed

Position

Mirror

B

D

Just before
reaching
this junction
check
Mirror
Signal
Position
Speed
and
Look

Look →

Speed →

Position →

Signal →
(right-hand
indicator)

Mirror →

Assess junction →

A

Correct positioning is vital when turning right. The situation illustrated calls for particularly careful judgment

3 'Do I need to adjust my distance from the vehicle ahead?' (separation distance)

4 'Is my speed correct?' (signs and road and traffic conditions)

5 'Am I staying on this road?' (advance direction signs)

6 'Is it reasonable to overtake?' (observation—forward and rear)

The answers to all these questions concern *position* and *speed*. This, then, gives us the full routine for dealing with a junction: *mirror* and *signal*; followed by *position—speed—look* at the junction itself; and then *position, speed* again. Get in the habit of using this routine at all junctions. It will serve you well.

How *not* to join a new road

It may be very tempting when turning right on to a wider road, especially when there is little traffic from the right, to turn and drive along the centre of the road in the hope that you can fit into a gap in the traffic coming from the left.

This is very risky for a number of reasons. First, you will confuse drivers behind you. Second, the road may narrow, or there may be junctions or islands in the road further along. Third,

Fig. 23
Timing the junction sequence

Drivers coming along road A and road B have very different problems of timing and observation before joining road CD

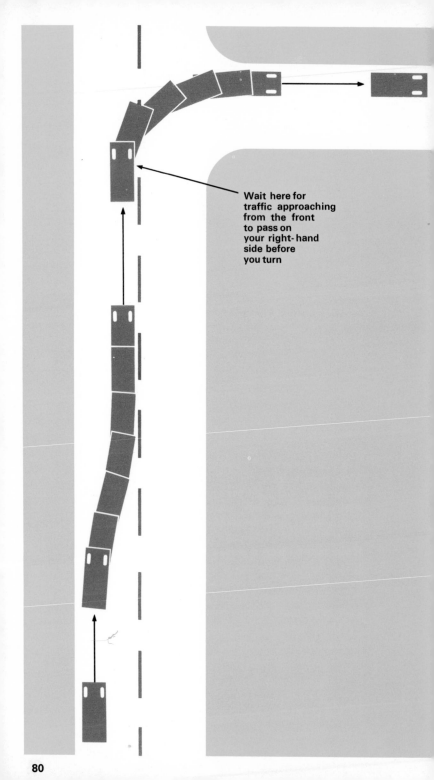

Wait here for
traffic approaching
from the front
to pass on
your right-hand
side before
you turn

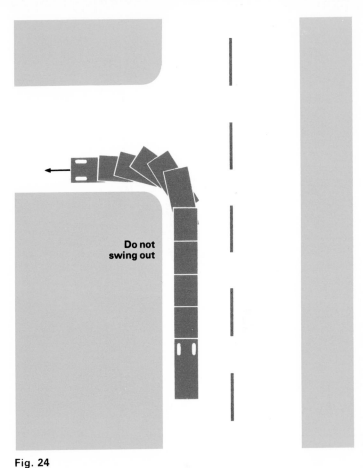

Do not swing out

Fig. 24

Turning right (opposite) and left (above) from a wide road
These two diagrams show the basic movements. Note the importance of correct positioning

there may be no gap for you to fit into. So don't create an extra stream in this way.

You may also be tempted to pull into the centre of the road and wait there to complete the turn. This, too, is dangerous unless there is a central reservation with gaps (as on a dual carriageway) or the road is specially marked to allow it.

Turning into a road to right or left

The junction routine we have described should be used at all junctions. Some of the steps are less important, others more important, according to whether you are turning into a road to the right or left. If, for example, you are turning right out of a busy road, there is the job of actually finding the turn you want. Giving your signal and getting into *position* in good time becomes

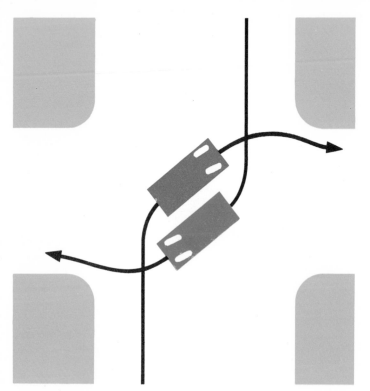

Fig. 25 (above)
Turning right (offside to offside)

Fig. 26 (opposite)
Turning right at a staggered junction (nearside to nearside)

At a staggered junction, as here, it is sometimes necessary to turn right by passing nearside to nearside. The disadvantage is obvious: each car blocks the other's view of oncoming traffic

essential—otherwise you may interrupt the traffic flow or even be forced to go on past your road. Looking, as always, is important. Don't begin a turn you can't complete. A sudden stop could have unfortunate consequences.

If you are going to turn to the left, watch out especially for cars parked, or about to stop, on the left. You don't want to get trapped behind them. Be very careful to look for cyclists or motor-cyclists coming up on your nearside.

If you are going to turn right, getting your *position* and *speed* correct is vital. You must look for traffic on the road you are joining as well as on the road you are leaving. Don't cross on-coming traffic until you can do so without causing it to change speed or direction. This will call for particularly careful judgment if the road is wide enough for two lanes of oncoming vehicles. Be

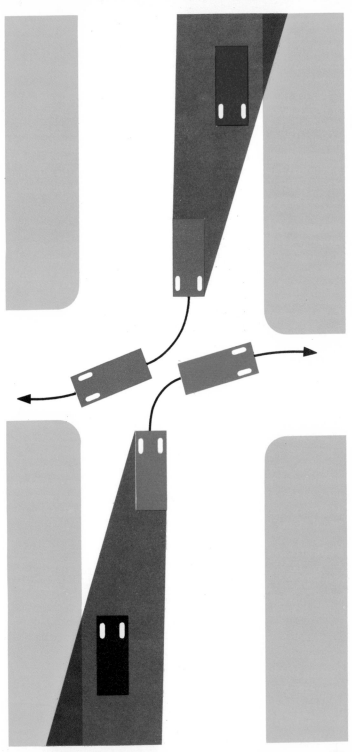

very careful where you stop and wait, because some of the oncoming vehicles may be turning right too. You may need to check the mirror again before starting to turn, particularly if you have had to wait. The correct positions for right- and left-hand turns are shown in Fig. 24.

Notice that Fig. 25 shows vehicles passing behind each other at a crossroads—or offside to offside. There are some junctions where the layout makes it more convenient to pass nearside to nearside, but this is less safe because each driver has his view of the oncoming traffic hidden by the other vehicle (see Fig. 26). The usual rule is offside to offside—but watch out for junctions where police control or road markings mean that you are intended to turn nearside to nearside.

Staggered junctions

At a staggered junction such as that shown in Fig. 26, you cannot turn right behind an oncoming vehicle that is also turning right (offside to offside). So be on the look-out for traffic hidden behind the leading vehicles—and be ready to stop.

Cutting right-hand corners

Fig. 27 shows what is meant by 'cutting a corner' when turning right. Always avoid this. It is dangerous because it reduces your zone of vision and puts you on the wrong side of the road.

When you are turning right out of a road which is only wide enough for one line of traffic in each direction, keep well over to the left (see Fig. 28).

Y junctions

These can be deceptive because some call for little change of direction. But if two drivers are approaching a junction on different roads, as shown in Fig. 29, and don't realise its importance, one at least will have to take very sudden—and therefore dangerous—action. Apply the PSL routine at Y junctions as you would at any other junction.

Pedestrians at junctions

Always be on the look-out for pedestrians and remember these two rules: *At pedestrian crossings controlled by lights or police* give way to pedestrians who are crossing when the signal to move is given. *When turning at a road junction* always give way to pedestrians who are crossing the road.

Fig. 27
Cutting right-hand corners
Three examples of bad driving:

A   The driver approaches correctly but steers to the right too soon

B   The driver approaches in the wrong position

C   The driver takes his line from the wrong kerb

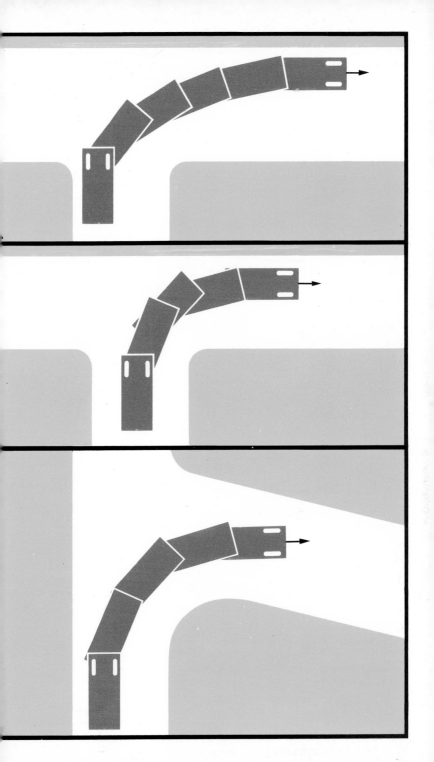

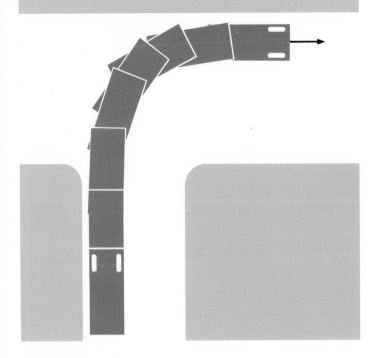

Fig. 28
Turning right out of a narrow road
This is the correct way. It leaves room for vehicles coming in

Dealing with roundabouts

Roundabouts help traffic flow by mixing together several streams of vehicles. But this very function creates a situation in which a high level of information and anticipation is needed. The rules to remember are: the GIVE WAY rule, which defines who should wait and who should move on; and the 'driving procedure' rules, which tell you how to approach the roundabout and what course to take in it.

Give way

The GIVE WAY rule says that when you approach a roundabout you should normally give way to traffic from your immediate right to avoid causing any approaching driver to reduce speed, to alter course or to be put in any danger.

Since this is a general rule, upright GIVE WAY signs (on posts) are not placed at all roundabouts but the points of entry are marked by single broken white lines on the road. Fig. 30 shows three typical arrangements.

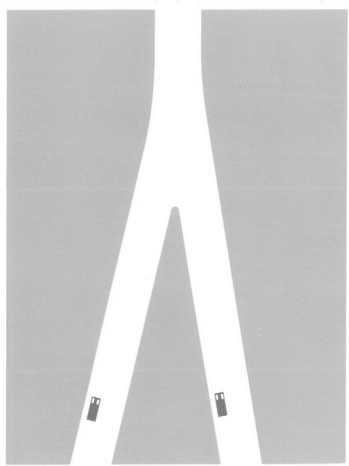

Fig. 29
Approaching a Y junction
Always apply the PSL routine as you approach the point where two roads merge. Failure to do so could force you to take hasty, and dangerous, action

Occasionally, although a junction appears to have a roundabout, drivers on one or more of the roads into it are given a clear passage. At these exceptional places the GIVE WAY rule may be applied to drivers *in the roundabout;* double broken white lines are marked across the road in the junction (see Fig. 31), and there are upright GIVE WAY signs.

Driving procedure
The following rules should always be observed *unless* road markings indicate otherwise *or* the approach road and the roundabout itself are quite free of traffic.

When turning left
Approach in the left-hand lane; keep to that lane in the round-

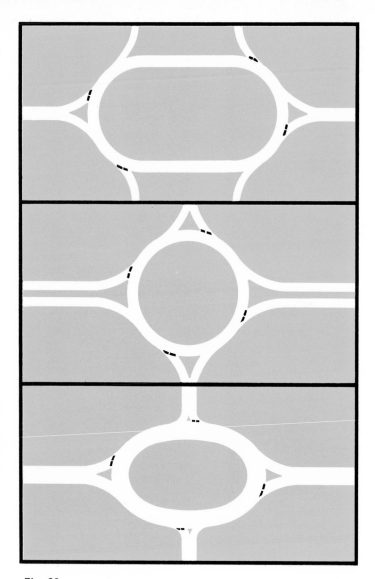

Fig. 30

Giving way at roundabouts

Typical arrangements, showing the entry points marked with broken lines (not to scale)

about and leave by it. Use the left-turn indicator on approach and through the roundabout.

When going forward

Approach in the left-hand lane; keep to that lane in the round-about. Use the left-turn indicator at the exit before the one you are going to take. If conditions dictate, approach in the right-hand

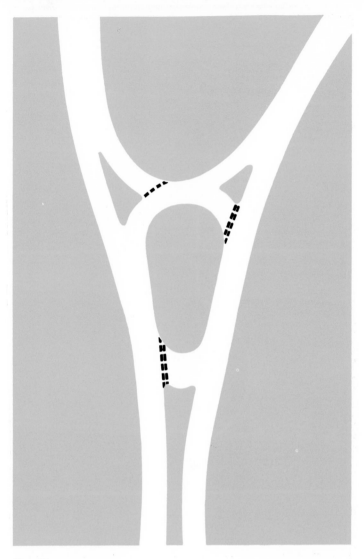

Fig. 31

Here, drivers *in the roundabout* are required to give way at two points marked by broken *double* lines

lane; and keep to that lane in the roundabout. Use the left-turn indicator at the exit before the one you are going to take.

When turning right

Approach in the right-hand lane; use the right-turn indicator before entering the roundabout and maintain this signal while keeping to the right-hand lane in the roundabout; change to

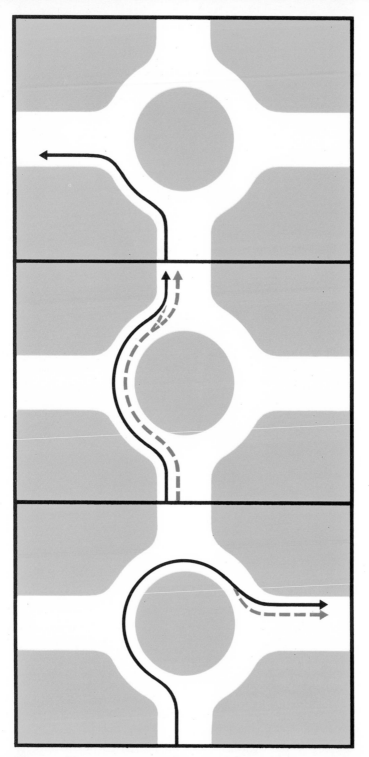

left-turn indicator at the exit before the one you are going to take.

Fig. 32 illustrates the correct courses to be followed including the proper choice of lane on the exit road. If you stick to these rules you will be letting other drivers know, by your course and signals, what you are going to do. And if they are observing the rules too, you will know what they are going to do. But note that they are not hard and fast. For instance, 'if conditions dictate . . .' means that you need to weigh up the situation and apply a degree of commonsense discretion. As we said earlier, roundabouts are places where traffic streams mix. So be prepared for other drivers to cross your path to leave by the next exit, and always be on the look-out for their signals. Watch out, too, for long vehicles—they may have to take a different course.

Where a roundabout has a very small central island there will be a sign (see Fig. 33) showing three white arrows forming a circle on a blue background to tell drivers that the junction is really a roundabout even though it may not look like one. There will also be arrows painted on the carriageway to indicate clockwise circulation.

Don't forget the other rules we have talked about: *mirror—signal—manœuvre* (MSM) and *position—speed—look* (PSL). You should apply these routines as much at a roundabout as at any other junction. Remember, too, that the signals for left or right turns must be given in good time so that other drivers are in no doubt about your intentions.

Summary

1

What to look for; deciding whether, and where, to stop before going on

2

Zones of vision; recognising obstacle points; ways to get a full zone of vision

3

How far forward? Far enough for a full view of the whole junction

4

The importance of careful positioning on narrow roads etc., and of not being too close behind the vehicle in front

Fig. 32

Driving procedure at roundabouts

These diagrams show you how to turn left, go straight ahead or turn right at a roundabout. The recommended course is shown by a solid line. If conditions dictate, follow the course indicated by the broken line

5

Judging the speed of approaching vehicles; looking out for 'dead ground'

6

Fitting in the routines—*mirror—signal—manœuvre* and *position —speed—look*

7

After entering a 'new' road; the need to use the mirror and adjust speed

8

Turning into a road on the left; signalling on approach; looking out for cyclists and pedestrians

9

Turning into a road on the right; signalling on approach; crossing other turning traffic

10

Roundabouts—the GIVE WAY rule; the drill for driving through a roundabout

8 Traffic signs

Signs are an essential part of any road and traffic system. They tell you about rules you must keep and warn you about what you may meet on the road ahead. Signs may be words and picture symbols on roadside posts, lines and other markings on the road, beacons, bollards or traffic light signals.

To do its job, a sign must give you its message clearly and early so that you will have time to see it, understand it, and act on it. In the past many signs were too small to read or difficult to see and there were too few of them. But this has changed, and there are now new-style signs.

In these new signs, symbols are used instead of words wherever possible, because they are more quickly seen and understood. Also, the similarity between our signs and those in the rest of Europe means that the British motorist on the Continent can understand the traffic signs even if he cannot speak the language—and vice versa.

The meanings of signs are much easier to understand if you know some of the simple rules about the shapes and colours used in designing them. To explain these rules, we will consider signs under five headings:

1 Signs that give orders
2 Signs that give warnings
3 Direction and other information signs
4 Road markings (which can do any of these three things)
5 Traffic light signals

There are also some special signs for motorways and other fast roads which we shall deal with separately in Chapter 14 under 'Motorway driving'.

Fig. 33

1 Roundabout circulation   2 Keep left   3 Turn left

Signs that give orders

Some of these signs tell you, as a driver, what you *must* do ('mandatory' signs) and others what you *must not* do ('prohibitory' signs). Most are in the shape of a circle.

Mandatory signs Most of these have white symbols and borders on a blue background. Examples are given in Fig. 33. Notice the difference between the KEEP LEFT and TURN LEFT signs.

You must also obey such signs as the circular one with STOP in white on a red background sometimes found at road works, and the STOP—CHILDREN sign (the 'lollipop') carried by school crossing patrols. This has black lettering on a circular, yellow background surrounded by a red border.

Two signs in this group have a special design which includes a red triangle, point downwards. They are the STOP and GIVE WAY signs. These two signs are always accompanied by road markings, and, because they are at junctions, they are important for your guidance and everyone's safety.

The STOP sign Fig. 34 shows the sign and road markings. Points to remember are:

Reason for sign Usually, that the junction gives so limited a zone of vision that you must stop in order to be able to look properly.

Markings The lines tell you how far forward you should go; in other words, they give you your final *look* position (in the junction routine *position—speed—look*).

What you must do You *must* stop. You must not then drive on and enter the major road until you can do so without causing danger or making drivers on that road change speed or direction.

The GIVE WAY sign: Fig. 35(A) shows the markings at a junction where there is a GIVE WAY sign at the kerbside. Fig. 35(B) shows an alternative arrangement with only the two GIVE WAY lines. This is used at junctions where there is relatively little traffic. Here are the points to remember:

Reason for sign GIVE WAY signs (or lines only) are put at junctions with major roads, unless they are controlled by STOP signs, traffic signals, or police, to show that main road traffic has priority.

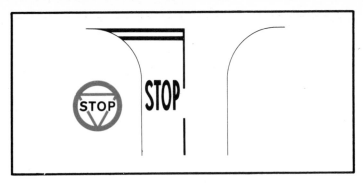

Fig. 34
STOP sign

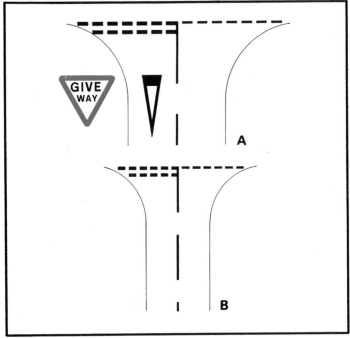

Fig. 35
GIVE WAY sign

Markings The double broken lines across the road show you where you must stop, if this is necessary, to take your final look.

What you must do Where there is a triangular GIVE WAY sign and lines across the road, you *must delay entering* the major road unless you can do so without causing danger to any driver on it or making him change speed or direction. If there are GIVE WAY lines only, you must still give way to traffic on the major road.

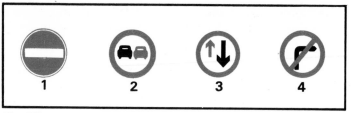

Fig. 36

Prohibitory signs

1 No entry   2 No overtaking   3 Give priority to vehicles from opposite direction   4 No right turn

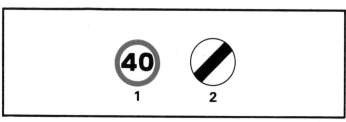

Fig. 37

1 Maximum speed limit   2 Maximum speed limit 70 mph

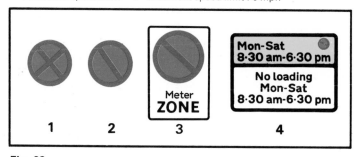

Fig. 38

1 No stopping ('clearway')   2 No waiting   3 Entrance to controlled parking zone   4 Restrictions on waiting and loading

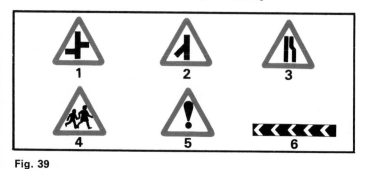

Fig. 39

Warning signs

1 Staggered junction   2 Traffic merges from left   3 Road narrows on offside   4 Children   5 Other danger   6 Sharp deviation to left

Prohibitory signs: These tell you what you *must not* do. Fig. 36 shows some examples. They are easy to recognise by their circular shape and red border. An exception is the NO ENTRY sign, which, although circular, has a red background instead of a red border. Another exception is the sign at the beginning of a lane reserved for buses.

The message is given either by picture symbols or by words and figures inside the red border. Sometimes the two are combined. Notice that the red symbols in the signs for NO OVERTAKING and PRIORITY TO VEHICLES FROM THE OPPOSITE DIRECTION show what you are *not* allowed to do. Similarly, a red bar across a symbol emphasises what you must not do (see the sign for NO RIGHT TURN).

Speed limit signs are an important example of prohibitory signs (see above); the 'Speed limit 70 mph' sign is also circular— plain white with a black diagonal bar across it (Fig. 37). Miniature versions of this sign are put on lamp-posts where the normal 30 mph speed limit for a built-up area does not apply. Similarly, miniature versions of the 40 mph sign may be put on lamp-posts. Lamp-posts without either of these signs are a warning that you are in a 30 mph area.

Then there are signs which tell you that you must not stop and wait at all, or that waiting is restricted in some way. In Chapter 10 we shall see that, before parking, a driver should always ask himself, 'Shall I be within the law?', so it is especially important to be able to recognise these signs when you want to park.

The general pattern for these signs is blue inside a circular red border. Examples are given in Fig. 38. The end of a clearway has the same sign as the beginning, but with the word END on a white plate underneath.

Where there are restrictions on waiting, the edge of the road is also marked with yellow lines. These may be continuous double or single lines, or a single dotted line. Short yellow marks on the kerb indicate where loading and unloading is restricted. Generally speaking, the more yellow paint there is the longer the restrictions apply. The actual times are shown on plates on posts or lamp-posts along the road.

Signs that give warnings

Warning signs tell you of dangers ahead. Their message is: take extra care and be ready to slow down or carry out some other manœuvre. Most warning signs (see Fig. 39) are triangular with a red border and a black picture symbol on a white background; some are rectangular with the message in white letters on a red background.

These signs warn you of some danger which you might not otherwise be able to see or recognise in time. The particular danger—a bend, hill, hump-back bridge—will be clear from the sign, but only you can decide what to do about it. What you cannot do safely is to ignore it.

Besides the obvious warning, these signs can give you other useful information. Here are some examples.

Junctions   These signs not only warn you that there is a junction ahead, but also tell you what sort it is; whether it is a crossroads, staggered junction or roundabout. Sometimes you can get information about the layout of a junction from advance direction signs. Notice the sign for merging traffic. This is really a warning of a Y junction. As more underpasses and flyovers come into use, so there will be more of these signs.

Narrowing roads   The warning sign in Fig. 39(3) shows which side of the road narrows; and every sign of this sort warns you against overtaking until you can size up the situation on the narrower stretch of road. Another form of sign for narrowing road is used where a dual carriageway becomes a single (two-way) carriageway, and here there is the extra message—watch out for oncoming traffic.

Children and schools   Signs showing children warn you of places such as playgrounds and recreation centres as well as schools. They call for extra care; children are apt to dash into the road suddenly. Where the sign relates to a school there will normally be a SCHOOL plate underneath it; or there may be a PATROL plate warning you of a children's crossing patrol some distance ahead. When you see these signs ask yourself if children are likely to be about. Is it their school arrival or leaving time?

Low bridge   However small your vehicle, this sign has a message for you too. It is to watch out for high vehicles coming towards you. They may have to use the middle of the road to get under an arched bridge.

Sharp change of direction   Black and white chevrons are used facing traffic at some roundabouts. They are also used where the road changes direction so sharply that a BEND sign would not be good enough warning. Another use is to show which way the main road turns at a T junction. Red and white chevrons are used where there is a sharp change of direction because of road works.

Hazard markers   Reflectors set on black and white posts are sometimes used to mark the edge of the road surface (carriageway) on embankments and hillsides. Sometimes they also show where the road narrows, or where there is an obstruction such as a bridge parapet or the corner of a building very near the edge of the road. The reflectors are usually circular but may be oblong. They show red on your left hand (nearside) and white on your right hand (offside).

Other hazards   The sign in Fig. 39(5) is used for any danger for which there is no special sign. It will usually have a plate underneath telling you that the hazard is, for example, gritting, tree-cutting and so on.

Directional and information signs

Directional signs   These help you to find and follow the

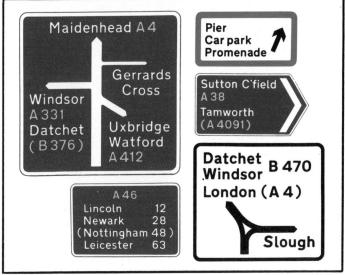

Fig. 40
Direction signs

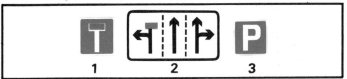

Fig. 41
Information signs
1 No through road   2 Appropriate traffic lanes at junction ahead
3 Parking place

road you want, or direct you to the nearest car park, station and so on. They are in different colours, depending on the importance of the road. Signs for important roads ('primary' routes), except motorways, have white letters and borders and yellow route numbers on a green background. Signs for other roads have black letters and numbers on a white background, and those for local places have black letters on a white background with a blue border.

Examples are shown in Fig. 40. Notice that each of the green signs is for a primary route; each has a different purpose. The first is an *advance direction sign* and you see this *before* you get to a junction. The second is a *direction sign* and this shows you the way to go *at* a junction. The third is a *route sign* to give you a check that you are on the right road *after* you have passed the junction. These signs also tell you distances and places on your route. Where there is a route number in brackets on the sign, this means that the road you are on leads to that route.

Information signs   These tell you where you will find parking places, telephones, camping sites, no through roads and so on. Examples are given in Figs. 40 (*top right*) and 41.

Road markings

Like other traffic signs, markings on the road give information, orders or warnings. They may be used with signs on posts or on their own. They have two advantages: they can often be seen when other signs would be hidden by traffic, and can give a *continuing* message as you drive along the road.

These markings help drivers to make full use of road space. Lane markings make lane discipline easier and so add to safety. Again the rule is 'the more paint the more important the message'. For example, a single broken line across the road at the entrance to a roundabout shows where you *should* give way to traffic from your immediate right; a double broken line across the road at a junction or within a roundabout means you *must* give way.

Single STOP lines A single continuous line across your half of the road shows you where to stop at junctions controlled by the police or traffic lights, at level crossings, swing bridges or ferries.

Lines along the road The most important of these are double white lines. There are three sorts: those where both lines are continuous; those where the line on your side is continuous but the one on the other side is broken; and those where the line on your side is broken but the other one is continuous.

There are two general rules which you *must*, by law, obey where there are these lines. First, no waiting on the carriageway. Second, where the line nearest you is continuous you must not let any part of your vehicle go over it, except to enter or leave a side road or premises on the opposite side of the road, or because of circumstances beyond your control. This does not mean that you must never overtake when the continuous line is nearest you. You may be able to pass a small vehicle like a motor-cycle without going over the white line. Sometimes there is room for two lanes of traffic one way but only one the other way.

Where the broken line is on your side of the continuous white line you can cross the lines to overtake if it is safe to do so and you can get back on to your side of the road before there is another continuous white line on your side. Watch out for arrows on the road. They often tell you that you are coming to double white lines. Don't start overtaking when you see them.

At some very dangerous places, such as sharp bends and humps, the two continuous lines may be some way apart, with the space in between covered by diagonal lines. This is to give an extra safety margin; the rule is for all vehicles to keep off these lines.

Single broken lines along the road either mark the middle of the road or divide it into lanes. Watch out for places where the gaps in the broken line become shorter. You will be coming up to a danger spot such as a junction, bend or island. Sometimes broken lines show the edge of the road, and when used in this way may change to a continuous white line where there is particular danger.

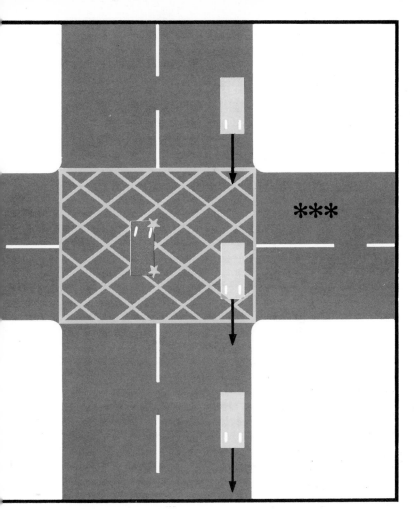

Fig. 42
Turning right at a box junction
Provided that your exit (✳✳✳) is clear, you may enter the box and wait there for a safe gap in the traffic

A continuous single white line is also used to mark the edge of a bus lane.

Cat's eyes Like hazard markers, cat's-eyes are red on the left-hand side of the road but white on lane or centre-of-road lines. On some motorways there are amber cat's-eyes marking the right-hand edge of the carriageway and green ones separating the deceleration and acceleration lanes from the through carriageway. In fog-prone areas the cat's eyes may be closer together. As with broken white lines, the nearer the cat's-eyes are together the more important their message.

Hatched markings Diagonal lines may be used to mark a

safety zone to protect vehicles waiting to turn right. Keep off these areas if you possibly can.

Box junction markings You should never enter any junction if by doing so you will block it. At box junctions, which are marked with yellow criss-cross lines, you *must not* go into the junction unless the way through, and the mouth of your exit from it, are clear. There is only one exception to this rule, and that is if you want to turn right and the way through to your exit is blocked by oncoming traffic. In this case you may wait in the area marked with yellow lines until there is a gap in the traffic which allows you to cross over into your exit (see Fig. 42).

Words on the road Words painted on the road surface, such as STOP, SLOW, KEEP CLEAR, and so on, usually have an obvious meaning. Where they indicate that a part of the road is 'reserved' for particular vehicles—buses or ambulances, for example—the message is 'Don't park here'.

Outside school entrances the words SCHOOL—KEEP CLEAR are used with zig-zag markings along the edge of the road. Again the message is not to stop or park on these lengths of road; they are places where both drivers and children crossing to and from the school need to have a clear view.

Another kind of worded sign on the road surface is the destination marking near busy junctions which repeats the message given on advance direction signs about towns and road numbers. These signs are put well back from the turn so that you have time to see them, and get into the right lane. They are especially helpful when the advance direction sign is hidden by a large vehicle.

Lane arrows These show you which lane to take for the direction you want to go. Where the road is wide enough for three lanes you may find each one arrowed for a different direction —the nearside lane for a left turn, the middle lane for straight ahead, and the outside lane for a right turn. Some arrows may be combined, depending on the amount of traffic using the junction. If the road is wide enough only for two lanes, the arrows have to be combined. Where there is a left-filter arrow at traffic lights, the filter (nearside) lane will be marked with the left-turn arrow and traffic going straight ahead or turning right will use the other lane, marked with a combined straight-ahead and right-turn arrow.

Left- and right-turn arrows are placed well before your turning point to guide you into the proper lane for turning. They are *not* intended to indicate the exact point at which you should turn. It is especially important to remember this at right turns.

Traffic light signals

Traffic lights have three lights which change in a fixed order: red, red with amber, green; then amber, and then red again. This means that when you see a traffic signal ahead you should know (as well) what the next signal will be.

The meaning of each signal is as follows:

Red means stop and wait at the stop line.

Red with amber means stop and wait. This is the safety margin for drivers on the other road to clear the junction and you must not go on until green shows.

Amber means stop unless you have already crossed the stop line or are so close to it that to pull up might cause an accident.

Green means that you may drive on if the way is clear. Take special care when turning left or right and give way to pedestrians who are crossing. Don't ever 'race for the line'. You must be ready to stop, especially if green has been showing for some time.

A green arrow means that you may go (filter) in the direction of the arrow. You may do this whatever other signals are showing.

Anticipation and the use of the *mirror—signal—manœuvre* and *position—speed—look* routines are just as important when you are coming up to traffic lights as at any other junction. Being prepared to stop, and getting in the correct lane—by paying careful attention to the lane markings—and the right gear, are specially important.

Traffic lights—either the red, amber, green or twin flashing red lights—are also used to control traffic where low-flying aircraft cross the road, at swing or lifting bridges and at other places. They must always be obeyed—twin flashing red lights mean STOP, of course.

Summary

1

Signs that give orders—what you must do; what you must not do. STOP **and** GIVE WAY **signs and lines**

2

Warning signs—how to use them properly; points to remember about particular signs

3

Direction signs—using them before and after junctions

4

Information signs

5

Road markings; double white lines and what they mean; words and arrows on the road

6

Traffic lights—when to stop and when to go

9

Dealing with hills

When a vehicle is being driven uphill the engine not only has to drive it along the road but lift its weight as well. Going downhill, the weight of the vehicle helps the engine to drive it along. In each case, the effect of the controls is different from what it is on the level. It is useful to look at the main differences and see how they affect your driving.

Going uphill (as compared with driving on level roads):

1 It is harder for the engine to make the car go faster

2 The brakes slow the car down sooner

3 If you reduce pressure on the accelerator, or if you declutch, your speed will drop much more quickly than it would on the level. A change down may then become necessary and this must be done briskly so as not to lose too much speed

4 When stopping, you can brake later and declutch later, but you must use the handbrake sooner to avoid rolling back

Going downhill (as compared with driving on level roads):

1 Generally, it is harder to slow down and the brakes have less effect

2 It is harder for the engine to slow the car down, and in the higher gears it will not do so at all

3 If you declutch, the car will run faster

4 Gear changes are more difficult and it is therefore important to be in the right gear before you begin to go downhill

We dealt with moving away uphill in the basic driving sequences in Chapter 4. When it comes to dealing with hills in the ordinary course of driving remember the following points:

Fig. 43
Warning signs
1 Steep hill upwards   2 Steep hill downwards

Going up

1 **Look for signs** The warning sign for a hill (upwards) will tell you how steep the slope is. The figures on it—say 1:6—mean that for every six feet (horizontal) the road rises one foot (see Fig. 43). The lower the second figure, the steeper the hill: 1 in 4 is steeper than 1 in 6. Extra signs on oblong plates may tell you the length of the hill or give you other information about it.

2 **Assess the hill** Weigh up a hill as you would a junction and change down in good time if a change is necessary. If you cannot see much of the hill because the road turns, *change before the turn* because climbing and turning at the same time mean harder work for your engine. Also traffic tends to slow on hills, especially at turns.

3 **Speed** Don't try to hang on to a high gear in an attempt to keep up your speed. Your car will climb better in a lower gear.

4 **Separation distance** Keep well back from the vehicle in front. If you get close and the driver ahead slows down for some reason, you may have to make a sudden stop. Holding back may enable you to keep going gently while he regains speed. This is not only safer but it can help to avoid congestion.

5 **Overtaking** Overtaking uphill is usually difficult. But where you are in mixed traffic on a straight upward gradient, perhaps on a dual carriageway, you might be able to overtake. But keep a look-out for others who are able to overtake easily, and don't balk them. One of the biggest dangers about overtaking on a hill (except on a dual carriageway) is that the traffic coming towards you downhill is nearly always going much faster than you are and is much less able to slow down or stop quickly (see also Chapter 11).

Going down

1 **Look for signs** The steep hill (downwards) sign is a warning you must respect. As with the uphill sign, it will tell you the gradient. But this is more than information—it is part of the warning. There may also be an accompanying oblong sign about using low gear.

2 **Assess the hill** Do this as soon as you can—the sign will help.

If you don't know the road, or conditions make it difficult to see, change down one gear right away and be ready for another change down if necessary *before* you begin the hill. (As with climbing don't delay your gear changes.)

3 **Speed** You will usually have to reduce speed to that of traffic ahead of you. Using your lower gears will help with this by giving you more braking power and control. The steeper the hill, the lower the gear.

4 **Separation distances** Leaving a good gap is important because if you follow too closely and the vehicle ahead slows down you will have to brake very hard—and the driver behind you will get very little warning. A good gap gives you time to slow down more gently.

5 **Overtaking** Overtaking downhill is safe only where there are no bends or junctions, where the visibility is good and you are *certain* that oncoming traffic will not be inconvenienced or endangered. Remember that just as you could not slow down easily, traffic coming uphill would have some difficulty in getting out of your way (see also Chapter 11).

Junctions on hills

When you leave a hilly road at a junction, or turn from a level road onto a hill, up or down, all the points mentioned so far become very much more important. Hills are not easy on car or driver and, as we have already seen, there are a great many driving operations to fit in when you go through a junction. Extra anticipation and considerable care are needed when dealing with a junction and a hill together.

Downhill junctions

When you are going downhill towards a junction, getting into the right position at the right speed needs the early use of mirror, signals, brakes, gears and steering. Remember the junction routine—*position—speed—look*. Your *look* will have to be made from a carefully chosen point at which you are ready to wait if necessary. Oncoming drivers will be climbing and, while their speeds may be easier to judge, you must be particularly careful not to balk them. If you are turning, don't move from your *look* position unless you are sure that you can complete the turn without blocking the oncoming traffic and causing a hold-up.

Uphill junctions

Again, it is important to judge your *position* and *speed* accurately when going uphill towards a junction, and to make correct use of mirror, signals, brakes, gears and steering. Your position will be particularly important to following drivers, especially if you are going to make a right turn. You will be very unpopular if you stop in the wrong position and force drivers behind you to stop unnecessarily.

Joining a hill at a junction

It is usually quite easy to turn left at a T junction into a road which runs uphill from the right. You can judge the speed of cars coming up the hill reasonably easily, and you don't have to cross any traffic stream. But if you are turning right and the road runs uphill from the left, you will find this much more difficult. Here you have to cross the traffic coming downhill from the right—probably quite fast—and at the same time fit into the flow of vehicles going uphill from the left without balking them.

Hills in town

What we have said so far applies to all hills, whether in town or country. But it is useful to look at some of the special conditions of hills in towns. First of all, there will be more pedestrians about. You need to take particular care at junctions when elderly people or young children are crossing the road uphill. Traffic speeds will be lower and vehicles closer together, making visibility that much poorer.

Traffic lights, school crossing patrols and pedestrian crossings will stop traffic on hills from time to time. This adds to the importance of using your mirror, recognising the sort of vehicle ahead of you, leaving a suitable gap when you stop, using your handbrake a great deal more than usual, and making sure that you are always in the right gear for the situation. You will be doing most of those things in towns anyway, but on hills they are all 'musts'.

Starting on a hill

Uphill Apart from the need to co-ordinate the use of accelerator, clutch and handbrake, as described in Chapter 4, there are two other points that are worth mentioning here.

First, because you must avoid balking traffic climbing the hill, you must apply the *mirror—signal—manœuvre* (MSM) routine carefully and without undue haste. Second, you must allow for the fact that your car will be slower in pulling away and gaining speed than it would on the flat, so you will need a larger gap in the traffic if you are to fit in safely.

Downhill This is a simpler operation because the weight of the car helps you to move away. (Faulty use of the accelerator, clutch or brake does not normally prevent the car from *moving away* on a downward slope.) But you must be careful to use the right gear for the slope of the hill to keep the car under full control. Remember, too, that drivers coming downhill from behind you will find it less easy to slow down or stop, so be sure that the gap is large enough before you move off.

Braking downhill

Don't rely on your brakes as the chief means of controlling your speed when going downhill. Overworked brakes get hot and may

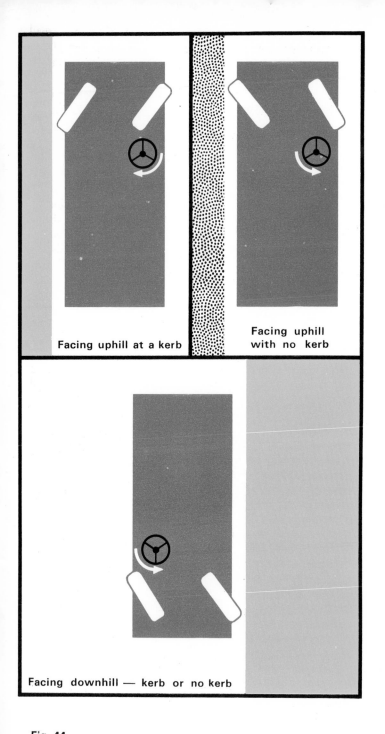

Facing uphill at a kerb

Facing uphill with no kerb

Facing downhill — kerb or no kerb

Fig. 44
Parking on a hill: how to set the front wheels

108

'fade' and lose quite a lot of their effect. Your chief means of controlling speed downhill should be the use of a lower gear; your footbrake should be regarded as an addition to your engine braking power in a low gear.

Get into a lower gear in good time and then be ready to slow the *engine* by braking the car with the footbrake. If the gear you are using is too high the *car* will run faster and speed up the engine. This is a signal to change down, but if you have left it as late as this you will have to brake very firmly to reduce speed enough to change down safely.

Because braking is best avoided on curves, use an even lower gear on a winding hill than you would on a straight one. You must do this *before* you begin to go downhill.

Parking on hills

It is far better not to leave your car standing on a slope. But if you can't avoid it, here are some points to remember.

Parking uphill Stop as close as you can to the nearside kerb and leave your steering wheel turned to the right. Then, if the car should roll backwards, it will be checked by the front wheel coming against the kerb. If there is no kerb, turn the steering wheel to the *left*. Then, at least, the car will not run back across the road. (See Fig. 44.) Leave the car in first gear—with the handbrake firmly applied.

Parking downhill Turn the steering wheel to the left, so that any forward movement of the car will be checked by the kerb. Leave the car in reverse gear and apply the handbrake firmly.

Parking with automatic transmission Whether facing uphill or downhill, make sure the handbrake is on firmly *before* using the selector setting 'P' (park). This avoids risk with some cars of a jammed transmission. If your car has no 'P' setting, turn your front wheels to the kerb (as above) and take good care to apply your handbrake firmly.

Leaving a gap Moving in or out of a parking space is more difficult on a slope than on the flat and tends to take more room. So leave a bigger gap—it will help you and others.

There are more details about parking in the next chapter.

A final word

Whether for power to climb a hill, or for braking to control speed downhill, it is always important to get into the right gear in good time.

Summary

1

The difference between driving on the level and uphill or downhill

2

Judging the hill; changing gear early; leaving a good

space behind the vehicle in front. The dangers of over-taking on hills

3

Junctions on hills; the particular importance of the *position —speed—look* routine; judging the speed of vehicles on the road you are joining

4

Special problems of hills in towns; the need to use the handbrake more

5

Starting on a hill; the importance of the *mirror—signal— manœuvre* routine. Picking the right gap to fit into

6

Braking downhill; the use of lower gears; using the foot-brake for *assistance*; braking on winding hills

7

Parking on hills; turning the front wheels to the kerb; leaving the car in gear; the necessity for leaving a larger space. Cars with automatic gears

10 Manœuvring

This chapter covers the manœuvres of reversing, turning and parking.

Before carrying out a manœuvre in a particular place, there are three questions you must ask yourself:

1 'Is this a safe place?'

2 'Is this a convenient place?'

3 'Shall I be within the law?' (The answers to the first two questions will probably help to answer this one too, because traffic law is based on safety and convenience. There may, however, be cases where the law forbids a particular manœuvre for reasons which, although good ones, may not be immediately obvious)

Your knowledge of the Highway Code, signs and other guidance and your own common sense will provide the answers. Then there is another question, the answer to which will depend very much on your experience and the vehicle you are driving:

4 'Can I control my vehicle accurately enough to use this particular place?'

Only you can answer this last question. For instance, if you are an experienced driver it may not worry you to reverse downhill for a reasonable distance. But if you are not so experienced you may feel unsure about reversing for even a yard or so downhill. The car you are driving and its steering circle may also influence your answer. But only when you can answer yes to all four questions can you be sure that the place you have chosen for your manœuvre is a suitable one.

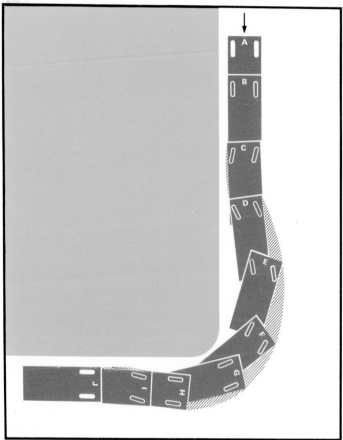

Fig. 45

The shaded part of the road shows how the car swings about as the steering wheel is turned. Most drivers take more room than this to reverse round a corner. At such close quarters a mistake could mean tyre damage against the kerb

A Start—with wheels parallel to kerb

B Moving back towards the corner

C *Very slight* right lock here will steer back of car away from kerb

D Back of car is now pointing away from kerb. Driver changes to left lock ready to turn corner

E More left lock now as the car is really beginning to turn the corner

F Some left lock is being taken off. Part of the car is round the corner—but not the steering end of it

G Less left lock now and more of the car round the corner—but still not the steering end

H The steering end is round the corner and all the left lock is off (wheels straight)

I Car moves very slowly while just enough right lock is put on to bring it parallel to the kerb

J Car is in position at the kerb

Reversing

Many manœuvres need reverse gear at some stage, so let us look first at the process of going backwards in a motor vehicle. Using reverse gear is obviously difficult for new drivers, not only because of the altered direction of travel but because the car steers differently; the front wheels become, in effect, the rear ones (see Fig. 45). When you drive forwards you can see the car turning with the steering. In reverse, you have to wait for the steering to take effect.

The first secret of manœuvring is to get the vehicle to move *slowly* enough. This way, the movements of the steering wheel will have the greatest possible effect. Don't turn the steering wheel while your car is stationary, but as soon as the car begins to move, however slowly, the steering wheel can be turned quite briskly. If your car has a small turning circle you will be able to change the angle of the front wheels quickly. The greater the amount of steering lock, the more important it is to move the car slowly. The second secret of manœuvring is to remember, all the time, which way your front wheels are pointing.

Reversing is not easy to master. Practice should begin with driving backwards in a straight line and then go on to turning corners and more complicated manœuvres.

How to sit

To reverse, you need to turn slightly in the seat. How much you turn will vary with your build and the car you are driving. When reversing straight back or to your left, you should hold the steering wheel with your right hand near the top (12 o'clock) and your left hand low on the wheel so that the rim may either slide through it or be gripped as necessary. If you find this position difficult because of your physical build or some other factor, hold the wheel at 12 o'clock with your right hand and sit so that you can steady your left arm on the back of your seat or along the back of the front passenger seat.

How to steer

One difficulty about steering, particularly in reverse, is to know just when to *begin* turning the steering wheel and when to straighten up. It is often helpful to move the steering wheel sooner than seems necessary. This, coupled with a slow speed, gives you time for unhurried control and time for checks to front and rear.

What to look for

Always check for other traffic before you drive backwards. Make quite sure there is nothing in your way—particularly children playing behind your car. Check all round—forwards, behind, over both shoulders and in your mirror. If you are in any doubt, get out (or ask your passenger to do so) to make quite sure. Keep a good look-out all the time you are moving backwards and always be ready to stop.

Before reversing, make quite sure that there are no children playing behind your car. If in doubt, get out and look

Reversing into a side road on the left

Fig. 45 shows how a skilled driver can back round a corner, keeping very close to the kerb. Most drivers will probably need a bit more room than this—not least because any misjudgment could mean tyre damage against the kerb.

Remember these points about this manœuvre:

1 Although you must watch the line of the corner, you cannot follow it exactly

2 When you have reached the point at which you are going to begin turning the steering wheel (C), check forward to make sure that your car will not swing out (D, E, F) into the way of approaching traffic

Fig. 46

Reversing to the right

1 Do not drive across the road until this point is reached—and then only after full and proper observation

2 Stop here, then reverse. Use a little left lock, then full right lock (compare with Fig. 45)

3 By about this point, the front wheels should have been straightened

4 Back well down the road, so that the normal position on the left can be reached well away from the corner

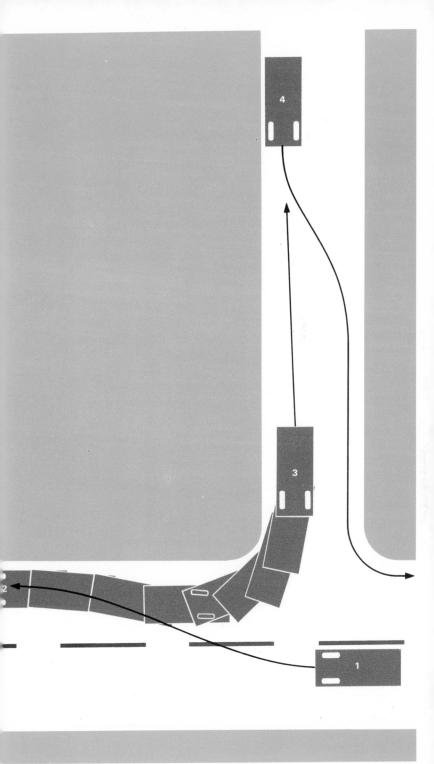

3 When you begin to see into the side road (E, F) look for vehicles coming along it

4 At the same time, be ready to start to straighten up your steering

5 Always keep to your own half of the road

Reversing into a side road on the right

This is a useful manœuvre when there isn't a convenient turning on the left, or you can't see very well through the rear window. Fig. 46 shows that it is, in fact, two manœuvres. The first is to cross to the other side of the road (after passing the junction). As with any other change of direction, this needs full use of your mirror and proper judgment of position and speed. You should also take the opportunity to weigh up the side road as you pass it.

The second manœuvre is the turn itself. Sit so that you have a good view over your shoulder to the right and can see forward and to the left. Don't forget these checks: they are even more important here than in the left-hand reverse. Fig. 46 shows you, in detail, how to position your car.

Some more points about reversing

Besides asking yourself the four questions at the beginning of this chapter, remember also:

1 Not to reverse into a main road from a side road

2 Not to reverse without making sure that it is safe to do so, even if it means getting help

3 It is an offence to drive backwards on a road for such a distance as to inconvenience other road users. So keep your reversing as short as possible.

4 Whenever you reverse you must be ready to stop and give way to other road users

Turning round

Every motorist has to turn round in the road at some time in his driving career. Here are three different ways of doing it.

Using a side road to turn and go back

This method is not so suitable for narrow or busy roads.

1 Find a side turning on your nearside into which you can reverse

2 As you drive past the side turning, look down it and weigh it up. Then stop just past it

3 Make sure the road is clear behind you, reverse round the corner. Stop close to the kerb, far enough back for you to be able to position properly for a right turn as you—

4 Drive forward, applying the junction routine (*mirror—signal—position—speed—look*) before driving out into your original road

An alternative way is to drive into the side road on the left and then find another turning to reverse into. Or drive into the side road and then turn round in that road, using the manœuvre we describe next.

Turning in a road by using forward and reverse gears

This is a useful turn in culs-de-sac and roads where there are no side turnings or openings to reverse into. The drill is illustrated in Fig. 47.

The various stages of this turn are as follows:

1 Choose a place where there is good visibility, no obstruction in the road or on the pavement, and where you have plenty of room

2 Stop on the left

3 Make sure that the way is clear in front and behind—give way to passing vehicles

4 Go *slowly* forward in first gear, turning your steering wheel *briskly* to the right. Aim at getting your car at a right angle across the road

5 When the front of your car is about three feet from the kerb and still moving very *slowly*, change the lock by turning the steering wheel *briskly* to the left

6 As your front wheels get near to the kerb, declutch and stop (footbrake). Put on the handbrake because of the camber or slope of the road. Select reverse gear

7 Make sure again that the way is clear. Back slowly across the road. As you do this, turn the steering wheel farther to the left—if it will go. Then, as the back of your car nears the kerb (you will see this over your right shoulder), turn the steering wheel *briskly* to the right so that when you stop you will be on the right-hand lock ready to drive forward again

8 Declutch and stop (footbrake). Put on the handbrake. Select first gear

9 Make sure that the road is clear and drive forward

10 You should then be able to straighten up on the left of the road. (If your vehicle is awkward to steer, or if you have had to turn in a narrow road, or where the camber is very steep, you may have to reverse again)

Finally, be careful if you let your car overhang the kerb. This can be dangerous to pedestrians and there is a risk of hitting trees, lamp-posts etc.

Making a U turn

This means turning your car right round in the width of the road. U turns are prohibited on motorways and in one-way streets, and on some other roads where there will be a sign—see Fig. 48—to tell you of the prohibition.

If you apply our four test questions about safety, convenience,

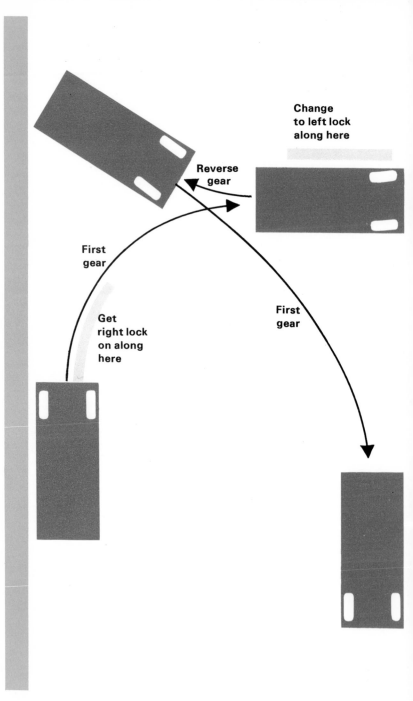

**Change
to left lock
along here**

**Reverse
gear**

**First
gear**

**First
gear**

**Get
right lock
on along
here**

**Fig. 47
Turning in a road by forward and reverse gears**

Fig. 48
No U turns

lawfulness and your own ability, you will see that a U turn isn't something you can do all that often. Nevertheless there are places where you can do it—and with some saving in time—such as little-used wide roads, or other quiet roads if your car is small or has an unusually small turning circle. But always remember that this is a manœuvre which other drivers do not ordinarily expect, so the safe routine of *mirror—signal—manœuvre* is particularly important.

Parking

Don't park on a road if there is somewhere else to leave your car. If you must use a road, choose a safe place. Before you leave a car anywhere, ask yourself the first three questions at the beginning of this chapter: Is it *safe, convenient* and *lawful*?

Some of the answers will be given by road signs and markings. These will tell you the places to avoid and whether there are restrictions at certain times or on particular days of the week. The question of safety will be answered by a knowledge of the Highway Code, which gives a list of places where you should not park, and by your own observation and common sense. Don't follow someone else's bad example.

Car parks

In a properly arranged car park there are markings to show you where to put your car. There are also arrows and signs to show the lanes you should take inside the car park. Always try to 'park pretty'; that is, squared up in the middle of the marked space.

In multi-storey, underground and indoor car parks, it is a good idea to use side lights whenever your car is *moving*—picking out moving cars among a lot of parked ones can be tricky in artificial light.

Unless you find a space at the end of a row, you will have to fit your car into a gap between two other vehicles. If the cars on either side are well parked you just have to centre your car between the lines. But if they are not carefully parked, make a check on the gap which is left for you before you move into it. You will have to leave enough room for you and your passengers to open the doors and, just as important, for the drivers and passengers of the cars on each side of you to open theirs. This question of room is all the more important with two-door cars.

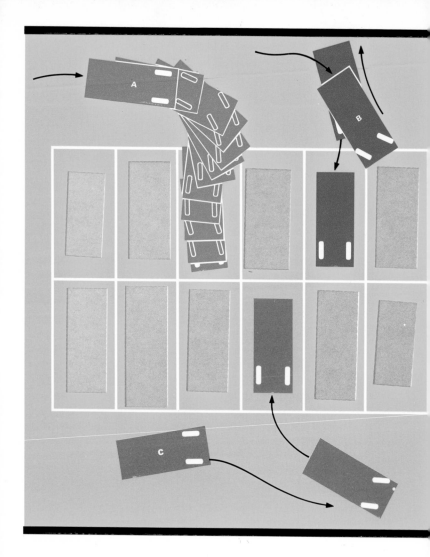

Fig. 49
Using a car park

A does a lot of steering at close quarters; even then he would do
    well to back out and straighten up

B gets neatly into place

C gets just as neatly into place, more simply, and is ready to go

Parking a car accurately needs care, skill and practice. Everyone
can be careful, but if you are short on skill or practice move your
car *slowly* so that the steering has maximum effect. You will also
have time to see and correct mistakes.

Sometimes the approach to a space in a car park does not give you enough room to 'square up' to it. Trying to get your car into a space in one go may involve very complicated movements of the steering wheel (see Fig. 49). A does a lot of steering at close quarters. He would do better to back out and straighten up as B has done. Better still, C has got just as neatly into place, more simply, and is ready to move out forwards. Car A made it in one go—but look at the position of the front wheels. Car B, on the other hand, nosed into the opening, moved back a bit, squared up, and drove in with the front wheels nearly straight. Except where cars are badly parked, leaving an odd-shaped gap to get into, it is nearly always best to reverse into a parking space, as C did. This gives you a better view when you drive out, especially important at night or if you have several passengers, and saves you from manœuvring with a cold engine. Even if you do have to manœuvre, you can do more of it in forward gear.

To sum up: before entering a car park use the mirror—and signal, if necessary. As you move forward, assess the park; notice its layout and markings, choose a space and see how other cars are parked. Use the mirror again, because car parks are crowded places and cars move quietly. Decide whether another signal will help, check your position carefully, keep your speed low and look again. Finally, 'park pretty', with your wheels straight.

Parking on the road

First, two general points. If there is a kerb try not to touch it when you park. Scraping the sides of your tyres will weaken them, with possibly disastrous results later. Secondly, don't leave your car so close to another that it will be difficult for you or others to get out again.

If there is plenty of room between parked vehicles you can, after using mirror and signal, draw into the side of the road and stop parallel and close to the kerb. But where the space between cars is not big enough for this, you will have to back in. You need a gap at least one and a half times the length of your car; even then you will only get in if you have a good steering lock (that is, a small steering circle). A gap of two car lengths will make the operation easier.

The most important step in this manœuvre is to go far enough forward before you stop. Drive past the gap and stop about half a length past the vehicle behind which you are going to park, parallel to it and about three feet away. When you have made sure it is safe to reverse you can then back into the gap, as illustrated in Fig. 50.

We have dealt with parking in some detail because it calls for care, and skill acquired by practice. If parking worries you, then practise it until you are really skilled. The advice given in this chapter should help you.

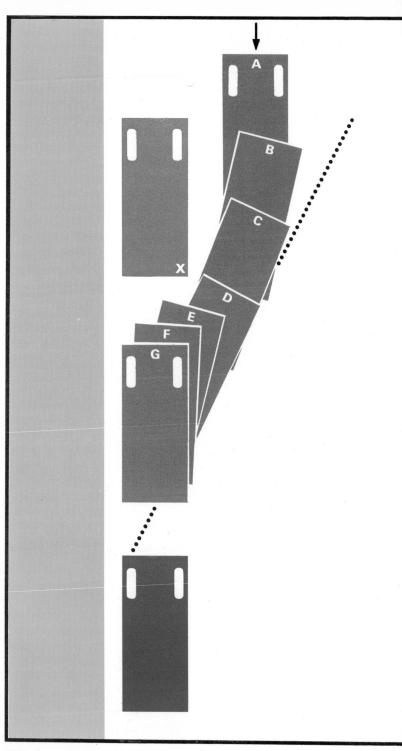

Fig. 50

Parallel parking in reverse gear. This takes advantage of a car's manœuvrability when driven in reverse gear. When doing this you will be something of an obstacle, so the *mirror—signal—manœuvre* routine is important. It is also vital to keep a look-out for passing traffic behind you

A Drive forward and stop parallel to, and not more than three feet away from the blue car. Then reverse with slight left lock

B Continue reversing with slight left lock but watch corner of the blue car at X

C Continue reversing but straighten front wheels ready to change to right lock

D As you clear the blue car, put on slight right lock and check the gap at X. Then put on full right lock. Your position here will bring the offside of the car in line with the nearside headlamp of the green car (see broken line in diagram). This should help you to judge your position and movements

E With a large amount of right lock, you will swing in towards the kerb

F Here you will be close to the kerb and the green car. Move the car very slowly and take off some of the right lock so that the front of your car does not swing in too far

G Check your distance from the kerb and from the blue and green cars, adjusting as neccessary

Before parking your car you must ask yourself: 'Is it safe ? Is it convenient ?' The driver of the second car to park in this road did not answer these questions properly, with the result that other cars have to thread their way through a narrow gap.

Summary

1

The questions to ask yourself before making any manœuvre: 'Is it safe—convenient—lawful?' And 'Can I control my vehicle accurately enough?'

2

Reversing: the advantage of doing it slowly; the proper way to sit and steer; making the right safety checks

3

Reversing to the left: where and when to look

4

Reversing to the right: where and how to look

5

Other points about reversing: don't back into a main road or for long distances; always be ready to stop

6

Turning in the road: reversing into a side road; turning with forward and reverse gears; making a U turn (and where not to)

7

Parking: off the road if possible. Car parks: keeping to the markings; going in backwards; parking on the road; reversing into a gap

11

The open road

Driving on the open road is largely a matter of putting together nearly all the advice in this book. Reading the road and anticipation obviously come into it. So do the proper and constant use of mirror and signals before making any manœuvre, and applying the proper routine at all junctions and other hazards. But there are some points which need special attention when it comes to open road driving, where speeds are usually on the high side, and these are dealt with in this chapter.

Stopping and separation distances

In Chapter 4 we talked about stopping distance and how this was made up of thinking distance plus braking distance. When driving on the open road it is essential to know and be able to judge your stopping distance at various speeds, because stopping distances get much longer the faster you go. So let's have another look at thinking, braking and stopping distances at speeds from 30 mph upwards, in good conditions on a dry road—and when conditions are not so good.

Stopping distances—in good conditions

When driving at	**30**	**40**	**50**	**60**	**70** mph
your speed will be	44	59	73	88	103 feet per second
your thinking distance will be about	30	40	50	60	70 feet
your braking distance will be about	45	80	125	180	245 feet
your stopping distance will be about	**75**	**120**	**175**	**240**	**315** feet

40 feet   75 feet   120 feet

20 MPH   **30**   **40**

Fig. 51
Stopping distances (red figures) get longer as speed increases
These are the stopping distances for a good car with good brakes on a

126

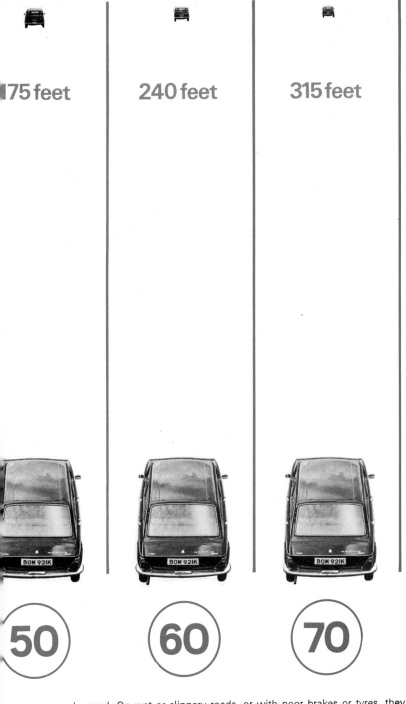

75 feet

240 feet

315 feet

50

60

70

dry road. On wet or slippery roads, or with poor brakes or tyres, they are much longer still

Fig. 52

The dial shows what miles per hour mean in feet per second. Note that you travel just about half as many feet per second again as miles per hour. In other words, at 20 mph you travel 30 fps, at 40 mph you travel 60 fps

Stopping distances—in poor conditions

When driving at	30	40	50	60	70 mph
you should allow					
about	150	240	350	480	630 feet

Have a good look at the second line in the first table (see page 125); it gives speed in *feet per second*, as does the speedometer in Fig. 52. You will see that when driving at 60 mph you travel almost *90 feet every second*. This means that if your thinking time is half a second (much better than average) you will travel about 45 feet—the length of three or four popular cars—before you are able to *do* anything about braking. Then on top of this there is the distance before your brakes can bring you to a stop. The faster you are going, the longer this will be. It depends, too, on road and weather conditions—if they are bad, you cannot safely put so much pressure on the brakes.

These drivers are heading for trouble. They are following one another much too closely for their speeds of 40 mph and over

There are two important points to remember about this. First, that your stopping distance is probably much longer than you think. Second, that, even with good anticipation, you will still travel quite a long way before you can turn the information you get from observation into action: and the higher your speed the farther you will go before you can start that action.

So the good driver uses anticipation continuously to give himself room to work in; room to recognise a developing situation and room to act. The action may be no more than taking a foot off the accelerator and covering the footbrake; or it could mean applying the full safety routine of *mirror—signal—manœuvre*. Whichever it is, smooth driving—the hallmark of the good driver—is the aim.

If you have to take panic action because you have insufficient room to act smoothly, you are either going too fast or driving too close to the vehicle in front.

How big a gap?

How much room should you allow yourself when driving in a stream of traffic? The absolute safe rule is to leave your stopping distance between your car and the one in front. But in heavy, slow-moving urban traffic, it is just not practicable to leave this sort of gap—40 feet (three to four car lengths) between vehicles moving at 20 mph—without a lot of waste of valuable road space

So a sensible balance has to be drawn. Even so, if you are driving closer than your *stopping* distance you are taking a risk. The gap should never be less than your *thinking* distance—if it is, you are heading for trouble.

But out on the open road and going at a fair speed, it becomes much more important to keep a good gap. A collision at speed can obviously have serious results. Most people drive much too close to the vehicle in front (many even closer than their thinking

Left:
How big a gap ? A yard for each mph of speed is reasonable in
good conditions. Here, the overtaking cars are about 70 yards apart

Below:
What a gap of 50 yards looks like when you are following a vehicle.
You are still too close if you are doing more than 50 mph

distance). So if, in future, you leave more room than you have
been in the habit of doing, you will almost certainly be doing the
right thing. Your stopping distance is still the only really safe
gap, but here again this is something of an ideal. A reasonable
rule to apply in good conditions is a gap of *one yard for each mph
of your speed*. (Do you know what 50 yards looks like when you
are doing 50 mph?) On wet or icy roads, or if your tyres, brakes,
or even your health, are below par, the gap should be much bigger.
And when a vehicle overtakes you and moves into the gap ahead,
lengthen the space again by dropping back.

Dual carriageways

These are becoming more and more common on main roads. A
division between traffic going in opposite directions certainly
helps vehicles to move faster and more safely, but there are a
number of special points to remember about dual carriageways.

Fig. 53

This sign warns you that you are coming to a single carriageway and there will be two-way traffic ahead

Use the lanes properly. (Have another look at the last part of Chapter 5.) Because traffic usually moves pretty quickly, it is vital to use the *mirror—signal—manœuvre* routine—and in good time. Keep to the nearside lane, except when overtaking (or in the few special cases mentioned on pages 141 and 142). Overtake only on the right. If there is a lot of slow-moving traffic in the nearside lane, there is no need to go back to that lane each time you overtake. It can be better to stay in the right-hand lane than to move in and out continually. But be sensible about this. Don't hog the right-hand lane and prevent others from overtaking you. Even if you are driving up to the maximum speed limit, it is not your business to stop others from going faster by staying in the right-hand lane. If the chap behind you is determined to exceed the speed limit, this could make matters worse by infuriating him and encouraging him to overtake you on your left.

When you are going to turn right to leave a dual carriageway, use your mirror, signal and move over to the right in good time. Be ready to stop in the gap in the central reservation. *If you do, stop clear of traffic on both carriageways*. Watch out for and obey any road markings in the gap—the general rule is to keep to the left in the gap.

There will be warning signs to tell you when you are coming to the end of a dual carriageway: look out for the TWO-WAY TRAFFIC sign (see Fig. 53) and the warning to REDUCE SPEED NOW. You will almost certainly have to slow down and your speed will probably be higher than you think, especially if you have been on the dual carriageway for some time. So check your speedometer.

If you are crossing a dual carriageway or turning right onto it, you really have two roads to deal with. The first will be one-way from your right and the second one-way from your left. At some junctions you have to turn left before you can cross or turn right onto the second carriageway. Whatever the layout, be ready to stop in the central gap—clear of the traffic.

Positioning is usually simpler when turning left onto a dual carriageway, but even then you must be careful not to swing out into the right-hand lane. Careful assessment of the speed of any traffic approaching from your right is essential. Incidentally, if you are on a dual carriageway and see a vehicle ahead waiting to join it from a junction on the left, it is helpful to move over to the

The driver of the red car is following through past the stationary lorry. He may think that the car he is following will protect him—but it won't

right-hand lane *if you can do so safely*. This will let the driver join the carriageway without undue delay, and also give you an added safety margin.

Overtaking

Overtaking in the wrong place or at the wrong time is asking for trouble and is one of the major causes of death and serious injury on the roads. This is not surprising, as you are usually on a collision course with traffic coming the other way. So it is vital to pick your place and time carefully; to be sure, before you over-take, that you can get back to your side of the road safely, without getting in the way of vehicles coming towards you or those you are overtaking.

There are two sorts of overtaking. One is where you are passing stationary vehicles at the side of the road (or even obstructions such as road works). The other is where you pass a vehicle going your way.

Passing stationary vehicles and other obstructions

This is usually fairly straightforward but, like any other driving

133

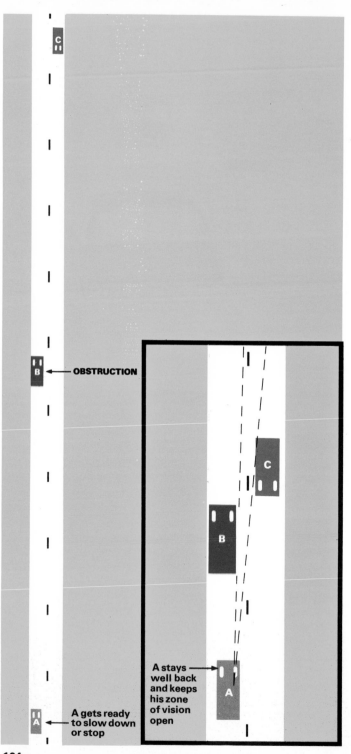

C

B ← OBSTRUCTION

A stays
well back
and keeps
his zone
of vision
open

C

B

A

A gets ready
to slow down
or stop

134

action, it needs thought. Fig. 54 shows a typical example. A can see the stationary vehicle or other obstruction at B on his side of the road. So the responsibility for deciding whether to go on or wait is A's. He should go on only if he can do so without making C slow down or stop. Otherwise, he must wait.

Put yourself in A's position. As soon as you sight B, use your mirror and then check that your speed is low enough to stop, if necessary, before you reach him. As you get nearer B, you can begin to assess what you see: whether C is slowing down or speeding up, whether B is still stationary or about to move away. Then you can make up your mind what you are going to do.

Having decided, check your *mirror* again, *signal* if necessary and then decide your *position*. If you are going to stop and wait, how close to B and how far in? If you are going to pass, how far out, and how soon to begin to pull out? Next, *speed*: is it time to brake for the stop, or to change down to move slowly towards B while C goes by, or to speed up and perhaps change down to, say, third gear to get briskly by? And finally, you must *look*—if you are stopping, to see whether it will be clear to go on after C has passed; or, if you are going on, to make sure that the situation has not changed since you made your decision.

If B is an obstruction such as road works you will also have to look out for workmen and their vehicles, and see what sort of road surface is ahead.

Obstructions on hills need special care. As we have already seen, gradients can affect braking, steering and acceleration, so you need an extra safety margin. Always try to act just that bit sooner on a hill. If you are going downhill and the obstruction is on your side of the road, begin your braking in good time. This will not only keep your driving smooth but will give drivers coming towards you a chance to see what you are going to do. If, on the other hand, you are going on, and perhaps accelerating, remember that if you should need to slow down again your braking will have to be that much heavier.

Finally, don't assume that you have right of way if the obstruction is on the other side of the road. It is much more considerate to let traffic, especially heavy vehicles, coming uphill have a clear run. You can start off again downhill more easily than they can uphill.

Overtaking a moving vehicle

Although you must pass a stationary vehicle in order to get on with your journey, you don't *have* to overtake a moving vehicle. So this brings up the first question to ask yourself: 'Is my overtaking really necessary?' If you decide that it is, you must then

Fig. 54

Waiting to pass an obstruction

It is difficult to see round a large vehicle, especially if you are too close behind it (*above, top*). If you keep well back (*above, lower*) you can see the road ahead and make sensible decisions

find a suitable place. Some places are never suitable, as the Highway Code shows us, and there are three main reasons for this. Firstly, you may not be able to see the road ahead; this happens at junctions, corners, the brow of a hill etc. Secondly, there may be a special need to allow for the movement of other road users; for instance, at pedestrian crossings, narrow roads and, again, junctions. Thirdly, when you overtake you are frequently travelling fast on the wrong side of the road for quite a long distance; this means that you cannot overtake safely unless you have a first-class zone of vision and are certain that you have weighed up all the foreseeable possibilities.

The speed of the vehicle you are going to overtake is very important. When you are coming up to a stationary vehicle, you know exactly where you are going to pass it (assuming it doesn't move before you get there). But when you are closing up behind a moving vehicle, it will cover quite a distance before you can actually pass it. How far it will have travelled will depend on the difference between its speed and yours. If you see a vehicle 200 yards ahead of you doing 15 mph and you are doing 30 mph, you will have to go 400 yards—nearly a quarter of a mile—before you catch up with it. This means that you must not only be thinking well ahead, but that you must be assessing and re-assessing the traffic and the situation, in front and behind, throughout this quarter of a mile.

This assessment has to be linked with another judgment about speed—that of any vehicle coming towards you from the opposite direction. Here it is a matter not of the difference between two speeds, but of the sum of them. Two vehicles coming towards each other at 55 mph will be closing the gap between them at 110 mph. They will get more than 160 feet closer to each other *every second*. So for every second you are going to be on the wrong side of the road you need, at these speeds, a pretty long stretch of clear road ahead of you. Overtaking takes much more than a second. And the smaller the difference between your speed and the speed of the vehicle you are overtaking, the more time and the longer stretch of clear road you will need. It is because so many drivers do not realise how much time and how much road they need to get past and back again to their own side of the road that there are so many fatal and serious overtaking accidents. Remember the golden rule: if in doubt, do not overtake.

Large vehicles present a particular problem, just because they are more difficult to see round. You need to keep well back to get a view of the road ahead so that you are ready and able to overtake as soon as a suitable moment arrives (see Fig. 55). You often see drivers bunched up behind a large lorry which they are unable to overtake because they are so close together they can't see that the road ahead is clear.

So play it right: leave a good space while waiting to overtake, and if another car fills the gap drop back again. You won't gain anything by sitting on his tail; you will only deny yourself the chance of having a good view of the road ahead, and help to build up a queue.

Another thing to remember about large vehicles is that their speed can vary quite a lot, particularly if they are loaded, between moving along on the level and going uphill or downhill. When you are behind a large lorry notice whether or not it is loaded. If it is you can expect its speed to drop, perhaps to a crawl, if there is a hill to climb ahead. But once over the top of a hill, a loaded lorry can pick up speed again very quickly, especially downhill.

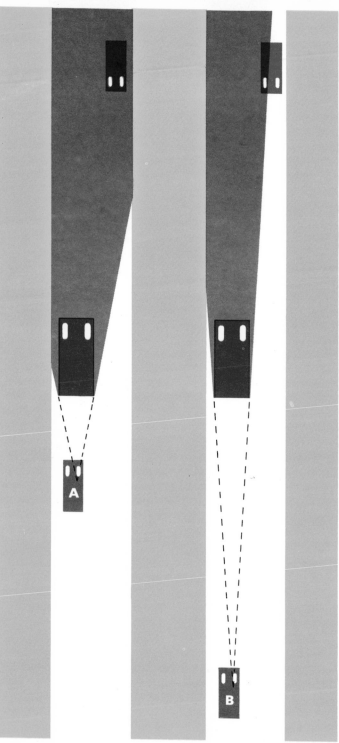

Remember these possible changes in speed differential when thinking about overtaking a lorry.

Other points about overtaking on hills have already been mentioned in Chapter 9—particularly that it is more difficult to slow down when going downhill; and that traffic coming towards you when you are going uphill will be approaching faster than usual. If you are overtaking uphill, give yourself time and room to get back onto your own side of the road well before you reach the brow of the hill. Your zone of vision will be getting shorter the closer you get to it, which means that a vehicle coming towards you could be on top of you very quickly.

On some long hills where the road is not wide enough for four lanes of traffic you will find double white lines dividing the road so that there are two lanes for traffic going uphill and only one downhill. In some places the line on the downhill side is broken. This means that you can overtake going downhill if it is safe to do so, but the uphill traffic in effect has priority (see Fig. 56).

Overtaking at the wrong time or place is particularly deadly on a road divided into three lanes, because the middle lane is used for overtaking in both directions. This middle lane is not an open invitation to overtake: on the contrary, it is most important here to make sure that the road ahead is clear far enough ahead. Never overtake when coming up to a blind spot like the brow of a hill; you could be on a collision course with a car which you can't see coming fast towards you from the other direction—and no sensible driver would want to do that. Many of these danger spots are marked with double white lines, so be on the look-out for advance arrows warning you to get over to the left.

On three-lane roads, junction signs and hatched markings in the middle of the road are particular warnings not to overtake. There may be traffic waiting to turn right or slowing down to turn left. So you must be ready to hold back.

Lastly, before overtaking anywhere, make up your mind what the driver in front is doing or is likely to do. He may be deciding whether he is going to overtake; or he may be content to drive at the speed of the vehicle in front of him. Perhaps he is going to turn off soon or can see something ahead which you can't. You can decide what he is going to do only by watching him—and the road ahead—for a while.

Fig. 55

Overtaking a large lorry

This diagram shows how getting too close behind a large vehicle makes it impossible to see far enough ahead. A's position is useless. B, who is keeping much farther back, has a much better view. If he moved *slightly* to the right, which he could do safely from this position, he would have a better view still

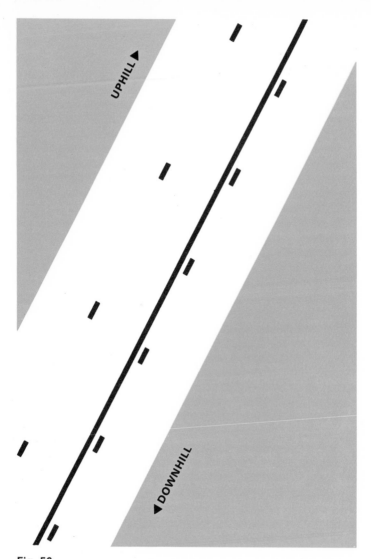

Fig. 56

Two lanes up and one down help overtaking up a long hill

Beware the driver ahead who is so close to the vehicle in front of him that he is constantly swinging in and out. He will be one of the impatient sort who doesn't give himself enough room to see ahead. Leave yourself plenty of room behind him—just in case he does something silly.

Steps to overtaking

Having looked at some of the particular problems of overtaking, we now sum up by giving the drill in detail. As you will see, it brings in the *position—speed—look* and the *mirror—signal—manœuvre* routines.

Position Near enough to the vehicle ahead so that you can pull out and overtake smoothly when you are ready, but not so close that you can't get a good view of the road in front of it

Speed Fast enough to keep up with the vehicle in front and with enough in reserve to be able to pass it quickly. You may need to change down to give you extra acceleration when you are ready to start overtaking

Look Assess the whole situation; in front, the state of the road, what the driver ahead is doing, any hazards, the speed and position of vehicles coming towards you, speed differentials and so on. Then the situation behind you, which means using your . . .

Mirror Never begin to overtake if another vehicle is overtaking you or is about to do so. When you are sure it is safe to overtake . . .

Signal Give a signal, if necessary, to show other drivers you intend to pull out. Even if there is no one behind you, a signal can be helpful to drivers coming towards you and possibly to the one you are overtaking

Manœuvre Make a final check in front and pull out on a smooth easy line. Get past as quickly as you can. Then another check in the mirror to see that you are clear of the vehicle you have overtaken and then pull in again to the left, also on a smooth easy line to avoid cutting in

You may have to do some or all of these steps several times before the right moment arrives. If, as you are about to overtake, someone overtakes you, then you must start the routine all over again. (Incidentally, never accelerate when someone is overtaking you.)

A last word of warning about overtaking. Many drivers seem to think that because the car in front has passed an obstacle or moving vehicle, it is safe for them to follow through. They seem to believe that the vehicle in front will protect them in some magic way. But it won't. The driver in front has more time to pull in out of the way of approaching traffic than you would have.

Always make your own decision about overtaking, based on what *you* see and what *you* know. The biggest virtue for any driver who wants to overtake is patience. If in doubt—hold back.

Overtaking on the left

Generally speaking, you should never overtake on the left. There are, however, a few exceptions to this rule. They are:

1 When the driver in front has signalled a right turn and has moved out so that you can pass him on the left. But make sure you do not get in the way of following vehicles coming up on your left. If there is a turning on the left as well,

watch out for anything moving into it across your path which may be hidden by the vehicle turning right

2 When you are in the correct lane to turn left at a junction

3 When there are queues of slow moving traffic, and vehicles in the lane on your right are moving more slowly than you are

4 When it is safe to do so in one-way streets

Level crossings

Level crossings with gates or barriers right across the road

Some crossings with gates or barriers across the whole width of the road are controlled by a gate-keeper or from the local signal box. The gates are closed to the road only when a train is coming. Where the crossing is not controlled, you will have to open the gates yourself. To do this, get out of your car, and look and listen carefully for any sound of a train. When you are sure that none is coming, open *both* gates and drive right across the railway onto the road on the other side. Then get out and shut the gates. Never stop on the crossing itself. At some of these 'open it yourself' crossings there are miniature red and green warning lights. If the red light comes on, a train is on the way. Keep clear of the rails until it has gone.

Crossings with barriers across half the road

Some level crossings have half-barriers which are worked automatically by approaching trains. As well as the barriers, this type of crossing has yellow box markings, bells, amber lights and pairs of red flashing lights at the side of the road. There are telephones to the nearest signalman at the side of the road near each barrier.

The first warning of a train coming is a steady amber light and the warning bell ringing followed by twin flashing red lights. Then, within seconds, the barriers come down across half the road. The train arrives soon afterwards. These crossings are designed to help the flow of road traffic. Properly used, they do this. But their safe use depends on everyone knowing how they work and keeping to the rules of proper behaviour. These are the points to remember:

1 Stop if the lights show (and the bells sound) as you approach the crossing

2 Never zigzag round barriers when they are down (or coming down)

3 Stop as close to the stop line as you can

4 Don't cross or enter the yellow box marking unless there is enough clear road beyond the crossing for your vehicle and any other one that you may be following onto the crossing

5 Keep a reasonable distance behind the vehicle in front so that if it stalls on the crossing you don't get caught on the crossing as well

6 If the barriers stay down and the lights continue to flash after a train has gone, it means another train is coming—wait where you are

7 If after about three minutes the barriers stay down but no train appears, telephone the signalman to find out what has happened

8 If you are crossing and hear the bells ringing (you won't see the lights, which will be behind you), keep going

9 If your vehicle breaks down or stalls on the crossing and you have passengers, the *first* thing to do, in *any* circumstances, is for you and your passengers to get out and get clear of the crossing. *Then* phone the signalman immediately. *Don't* waste time trying to restart, or trying to drive off on the starter before you get your passengers out or before you have phoned. If the signalman says there is no train approaching, try to restart your vehicle or push it off the crossing. Phone the signalman again as soon as you have done so.

10 If you break down on the crossing when you are alone in your car, try to start it again. But don't waste time. If you can't move it quickly, phone the signalman.

11 If the bells start to ring or the lights show or the barriers come down while your vehicle is still stuck on the crossing, get right away from the railway tracks—and see that everyone else does so too.

Open level crossings

Some crossings without gates have flashing red lights as at half-barrier crossings. The rule is the same: don't cross when the lights are flashing. In very quiet places there are crossings with neither gates nor traffic signals. Here you should slow down as though you were approaching a crossroad, look both ways, listen carefully and cross only when you are sure it is safe.

Summary

1

Driving on the open road; the need for reading the road and anticipation; the constant use of mirrors and of the safe and junction routines

2

The importance of knowing your stopping distances and being able to judge them accurately; making allowance for bad weather conditions

3

Keeping good separation distances—how big a gap; enough room to work in; the importance of driving smoothly

4

Dual carriageways; the proper use of lanes; keeping to the left except when overtaking; how to join and cross them

5

Overtaking; picking the right time and place; passing stationary and moving vehicles; looking well ahead; the importance of judging speeds accurately; avoiding queues; how to pass large lorries. Overtaking on hills, three-lane roads and, exceptionally, on the left

6

A drill for overtaking

7

Level crossings

12

Other people

Previous chapters have shown how much the good driver needs to watch other road users to decide on his own course of action and how important it is to fit in with the flow of traffic at junctions, roundabouts and so on. But 'other road users' means more than just the flow of traffic; it means everyone who is on or near the stretch of road you are on.

The good driver not only has to recognise what the other chap is doing or going to do, but must also understand his problems and difficulties and allow for them. To everyone else, we are the 'other people' and are grateful for help and consideration from them. Here are some general points which can help you to help others.

Emergency vehicles

If you see the flashing blue lights of ambulances, fire engines or police vehicles, or hear their warning, give way to them and stop if necessary.

Cars and lorries

Large vehicles ahead turning left As well as keeping well back from a large vehicle, remember that its driver may not be able to turn left without going out to the right first. So be very careful about moving up on the left; if you get so close that you cannot see his signals you may get caught out. Goods vehicles often have to turn into gateways and yards on the nearside, and the narrower the opening the more likely it is that the driver will have to go out to the right first. So watch out for these vehicles turning left, especially if they are long ones or articulated. Be ready to stop to give them room—and don't try to get past on the left—you could get caught.

Standing vehicles We have already looked at most of the problems caused by stationary vehicles. No road is wider than the gap between a stationary vehicle and the kerb opposite. The real message of a stationary vehicle on the road, however far ahead, is 'road narrows' (see Fig. 57).

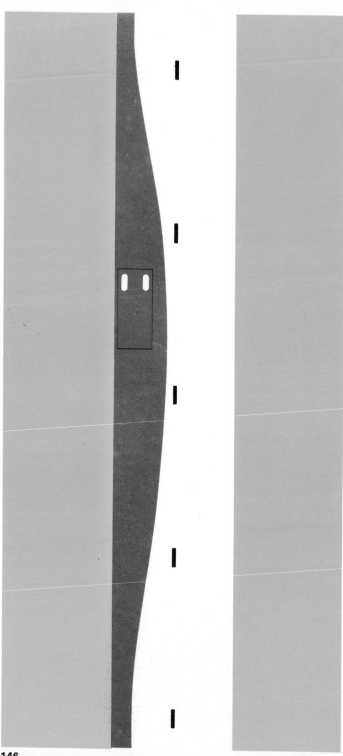

Be prepared for large vehicles to move out to the right before turning left

Gaps for turning vehicles You can often help other people (and yourself, in the long run) by stopping a little short to allow space for other vehicles to turn while you are waiting. At traffic lights, for example, a line of waiting vehicles may overlap a side turning farther back (see Fig. 58). Leaving a gap costs you nothing; it is not only good manners but it will reduce congestion. If you are waiting at A and there is a vehicle immediately ahead, leaving no gap, you can sometimes let a waiting driver turn in or out ahead of you by holding back when the gap does open. There are no rights of way about this; it is a matter of anticipation and fitting your actions to the circumstances.

Behaviour at junctions You may know how to deal with a junction properly, but other drivers don't know that you know. An eyes-down, last-minute-braking approach to a junction is not only bad driving in itself, but can alarm other drivers and lead them into panic action. Your actions should speak for themselves. A well-controlled approach to a junction tells everyone that you are aware of the situation and are dealing with it properly.

Cutting in To cut in is to force yourself into a stream of traffic in such a way that another driver has to get out of your way. It's a bad fault, most often caused by ill-judged overtaking or an unsuccessful attempt to pass which forces the driver to get back in lane regardless. If you see this situation building up, you can help to prevent an accident by being ready to drop back. Follow

Fig. 57

A standing vehicle tells you: 'road narrows'

Because the shaded part is lost, road width may be down to half

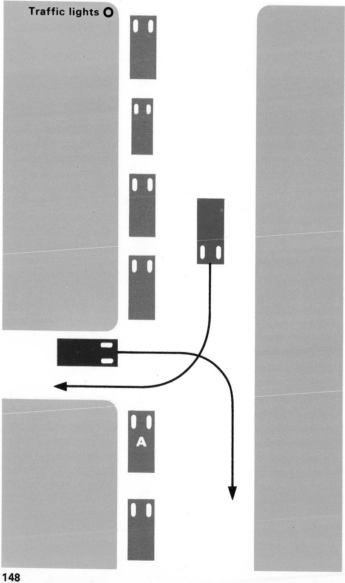

Traffic lights

A

the overtaking routine properly yourself, and you will avoid any need to cut in.

Left-turn indicators at a junction While waiting to emerge at a junction, you often see a vehicle coming from the right showing a left-turn indicator. Don't assume that it *will* turn left. Wait and be sure. The driver *may* be going to turn left; but he may also be going to stop on the left either before or after he gets to the junction—or he may have forgotten to switch off his indicators. If the vehicle is a large one it may be hiding others coming up much faster behind it, or even overtaking it.

Passing places on single-track roads If a passing place is on the left-hand side of the road, pull into it and wait to allow the overtaking or approaching vehicles through. If the passing place is on the right-hand side of the road, wait just opposite to it to allow other vehicles to use the passing place.

Buses and coaches

Look for bus and coach stopping places so that you will be ready to pull in, stop or pull out. Notice the design of bus shelters and stops so that you can spot them quickly, wherever you are. At busy times when bus traffic is heavy, there is a particular need to be ready to allow for buses stopping or pulling out—so use your mirror frequently and keep your speed well in hand.

When driving behind a bus or coach watch for passengers moving towards the door. This will often warn you of a stop ahead. Similarly, if you are held up behind one of these large vehicles at a stop and are thinking about whether to pass or wait, a rough count of the waiting passengers will sometimes help you to decide.

Remember that the bus or coach driver, although helped by sitting higher than you, has a much larger vehicle to handle and is handicapped by poorer vision behind him. So be patient, especially if there are several buses together.

Bus lanes In some towns there are particular lanes reserved for buses only. These are indicated by signs and road markings. All other vehicles (except, in some cases, cycles and taxis) are prohibited from using these bus lanes.

Near roundabouts and other junctions remember that a bus or coach is more difficult to manœuvre than a car. For a number of reasons, a change of lane will take more time and space for a bus than for you.

Cyclists

Look out for cyclists and make allowances for the differences between your means of travel and theirs. The younger they are the more closely you should watch them and be ready to slow

Fig. 58
Leaving a gap for turning vehicles

down or stop. A cyclist glancing round is a signal to you that he may be going to move out or turn.

Cyclists may make sudden sideways movements; give them plenty of room when you pass them.

Cyclists are affected by cross-winds, particularly at side turnings, near tall buildings or at such places as low bridges.

In headwinds or in wet weather cyclists tend to keep their heads down. This creates risk; be alert for it and for the danger of cyclists skidding (side-slipping) on smooth wet surfaces.

Cyclists going uphill have difficulty. Be ready for them to slow down or to stop and get off.

Cyclists with bulky loads Cyclists are sometimes tempted to ride when carrying light but bulky objects. This can seriously affect their control and balance and even their vision. So be wary.

Before turning left, look out for cyclists moving up between you and the kerb

When you are going to turn left, and especially if you have to wait at the corner, look out for cyclists who may have moved up between you and the left-hand kerb (or who may be using a cycle-track).

Motor-cyclists (including moped and scooter riders)

Much of what we have said about cyclists applies also to motor-cyclists, although some of them will be less affected by weather conditions and hills. There are many situations in which a two-wheeled machine is less stable than a car, so leave plenty of room, especially for riders on less powerful machines.

In many places motor-cyclists will be able to go on when there is no room for your car. Don't let this irritate you or encourage

you to push forward when you shouldn't. As with cyclists, be on the look-out for motor-cyclists who move up on your left when you are preparing or waiting to turn left.

Pedestrians

Pedestrians are not just 'traffic'—they are people, and the younger they are the faster they are likely to move or change direction. Those with prams, the elderly, the blind and the infirm all need your special care and consideration. They depend on you for their safety.

When you choose a place to stop and park your car, give a thought to pedestrians. Might it prevent a mother from getting her pram up or down the kerb? Would its position puzzle or confuse a blind person—for instance, by overhanging the kerb or blocking his path?

In busy shopping areas, watch out for pedestrians stepping out between parked cars. This is especially common in wet weather when shoppers are apt to make a sudden dash across the road

Turning corners Always give way to people who are already in the road when you turn a corner.

On country roads where there are no footpaths pedestrians, perhaps with children, a pram or an animal, may be coming towards you on your side of the road on a left-hand bend. Be on the look-out and keep your speed down. Remember too that cyclists become pedestrians on hills which are too steep to ride up.

Where vehicles are parked at the kerb or held up in a traffic stream, watch out for pedestrians who may step out between them. Elderly people and children are apt to do this and it is common in shopping streets, especially in wet weather. So keep

153

At pedestrian crossings give way to anyone with a pram

your eyes open and *keep your speed down*. Nearly a quarter of all pedestrian accidents happen near parked vehicles.

Don't use your horn too close to a pedestrian who appears not to have seen you. A quick tap, in good time, is best. If he has already moved out of your path, don't sound the horn at all. It could startle him into stepping back. On this point of considering others, don't use the starter and rev your engine just as an elderly pedestrian is level with you, especially when streets are slippery. Wait a second; it can make all the difference.

Pedestrians at crossings

People on foot have certain rights of way at pedestrian crossings but they are safe only if drivers keep to the rules and do the right things. Never overtake when you are approaching any sort of pedestrian crossing, and have your speed well in hand so that you are ready to slow down or stop to give way to pedestrians.

Zebra crossings Uncontrolled (zebra) crossings have flashing yellow beacons as an advance warning. The crossing itself is marked by black and white stripes. New zig-zag markings are being laid on both sides of the crossing, together with a give-way line about a yard from the crossing which marks the place at which drivers should stop for pedestrians.

The zig-zags make crossings easier for drivers to see. Over-taking the leading vehicle is prohibited on the *approach* side of the crossing, and parking or waiting is prohibited on *both* sides of the crossing within the area marked by the zig-zags. Pedestrians should not cross the road within this area, except on the crossing itself—but don't rely on this.

You must allow free passage to any pedestrian on the crossing. The approach to a pedestrian crossing is another place where the *mirror—signal—manœuvre* routine needs to be applied. Another thing to remember is that the 'signal' part means the arm signal for slowing down or stopping. The Highway Code tells pedestrians to allow drivers ample time to give way, especially if the road is wet or icy. A good practical rule for drivers is: Where people are waiting on the pavement, let them wait; but where they are crossing, let them cross. As with many good rules, there is an important exception and this is where a mother is waiting at the kerb with a pram. She cannot safely stand on a crossing holding a pram, but let her cross just the same. Remember, too, that in busy traffic some pedestrians—particularly the elderly and children—may be reluctant to venture onto a crossing. In this situation, it is courteous to stop if you can do so safely, and give them a chance.

Some zebra crossings are divided by a central island, and then each half forms a separate crossing.

At pedestrian crossings, controlled by light signals, or the police, you must give way to people who are still crossing when you get the signal to move. At some crossings, where pedestrians can use push-buttons to start the signal sequence, you will not see the red-with-amber signal before the green. Instead, there will be flashing amber. This means that you must give way to pedestrians on the crossing, but otherwise you can go on.

All pedestrian crossings should be left free during traffic hold-ups. Stop before you reach the crossing if you can see that you won't be able to clear it.

Wherever there are pedestrians:

1 Give yourself more time to stop if the road is wet or icy
2 Always give children, the elderly, the blind or infirm plenty of time to cross the road
3 Never signal to pedestrians that you are giving way to them. (There is no authorised signal for this, and it is dangerous to wave invitations to them to come into the road because you cannot be sure what other drivers may do)
4 Stick to the rules, then everyone knows what to expect

Children

The very young lack experience of traffic, and even the older ones are unlikely to be good judges of speed and distance. They are all apt to do things unwisely and without warning. So whenever you see a child on the footpath or the road—take *extra* care. You have to do for children what they may not yet be able to do for themselves—take proper care. Even if they show every sign of staying on the path, remember that they may dash into the road without warning. Over 800 children are killed on the roads each year and there are no more useless words than 'I didn't have a chance'.

Young pedestrians Although children are trained at school and elsewhere to walk on the footpath and to use pedestrian crossings, they do forget. So watch them carefully as you approach and as you pass be ready to stop. Give them plenty of time on crossings.

Children at play Children playing near roads are especially likely to forget the traffic. Think for them, particularly near ice-cream vans, window displays, street traders' stalls and so on.

A child running is a signal of danger to the child himself, to you and your passengers, and to drivers who may be following you. Be ready to take action *in good time* so that you don't have to brake suddenly.

Child cyclists Children on bicycles need plenty of room. Give them a wide berth when you are passing and always be ready in case they wobble or change direction suddenly.

School times Get to know school times in your area; these are the danger periods for children. Watch out for children on foot or on cycles, especially on dark winter mornings and afternoons. Keep a look-out for school buses, particularly in country districts.

Warning children of your approach Children often take more notice of a repeated tap-tap on the horn than they do of a loud blast, which can go 'over their heads'.

Reversing The Highway Code warns you to make sure that there are no children behind your vehicle before you reverse it. Make sure—even if it means getting out to look.

Children as passengers Children are safer in the back. Make sure that they are *seated* and, if they are old enough, that they wear a proper safety harness or seat belt. If they are not old enough for this, they should be held by a passenger who is wearing a belt or harness, or fastened in a cot which is itself firmly fixed. Be specially careful to lock the doors, and teach your children not to fiddle with locks.

Animals

The animals you are most likely to meet on the road can be divided into two groups: dogs and cats in towns and cities; and horses, cattle, sheep and led animals in smaller towns and the countryside.

Dogs When you see a dog, notice whether it is on a lead. If it is not (or if you can't see for sure) use your mirror and then keep an eye on the dog. If it runs into the road do your best—but don't swerve or stop regardless and endanger other people.

Cats can usually look after themselves but they do sometimes make a high-speed dash across the road. Be ready to ease your foot off the accelerator pedal—but no emergency stops.

Horses When you see a horse and rider, slow down, avoid making unnecessary noise, and leave plenty of room. A group of riders may mean a riding school and children learning, so go easy and be ready to stop or crawl past. If you see a string of horses near racing stables, look for signals from the first and last riders. Led

Opening a car door without due care can maim or kill a passing cyclist

horses may be coming towards you on your side of the road; be prepared for this, especially on left-hand bends in horse-riding country.

Other animals Always reduce speed and be ready to stop. Be patient, even if animals block the road while they are being moved, and respect the signals of the person in charge of them.

Signs about animals In some areas you will see warning signs about ponies, deer or other animals which may come onto the road. Watch out for them, especially at dawn or dusk and other times when it is difficult to see—in dazzling sunshine, mist and heavy rain.

Animals at night Look out for any lights which may warn you of animals on the road. Herdsmen sometimes rely on the lamps of their own bicycles.

The dog in your car If you take a dog with you train him not to clamber about. If you can't do this, tie him up. At all events—no climbing about and no touching the driver.

Car doors

Closed doors won't hurt anyone. Open, they can be a menace and can even kill a passing cyclist. When you stop, always link *doors*, *cyclists* and *pedestrians* in your mind.

Opening doors on the pavement side of the car can be a real danger to pedestrians, especially the very young or the elderly.

Don't open your driving door without first using your mirror and looking round to double-check behind. Even then, open it carefully.

With a four-door car, make a rule that no one inside the car should open the rear door nearest the traffic.

If there are children in the car, have some rules about who opens any door—and when.

Summary

1

Making allowances—emergency vehicles; large vehicles ahead turning left; standing and turning vehicles; passing places

2

Buses and coaches; making allowances for them; stopping places; bus lanes

3

Cyclists and motor-cyclists; why they need plenty of room

4

Consideration for pedestrians; correct procedure at crossings

5

The need to be especially careful where children are about; making them safe as passengers

6

Dealing with cats, dogs and other animals

7

The need for care when opening car doors

13 Keeping your grip

Tyres

The tyres of your car are, or should be, your only contact with the road. The area of contact is small—little more than the size of the sole of a man's shoe for each tyre. This chapter shows just how hard that small area of tyre has to work and what you can reasonably expect it to do for you.

Tyres won't do their job properly and safely unless they are in good condition—and this includes the spare. They can easily be damaged and, of course, they wear out. So they need to be treated with care, as well as checked, maintained and replaced when necessary.

How to save wear and tear

Keep your tyres at the correct pressures. Few things wear them out more quickly than running them too soft. This allows too much flexing, or bending, of the tyre walls (sides) and so makes the tyre overheat. Wherever possible, avoid driving through potholes and breaks in the road surface. If you can't avoid it—for instance, where the road is being repaired—you will save wear and tear by slowing down. Don't drive over kerbs or scrape your wheels along them when manoeuvring. This can cause damage to the walls of the tyres and lead to tyre failure later on. You can also save wear on the treads by avoiding high speeds, fast cornering and heavy braking.

Tyre pressures

Except for the obvious flat, you can't guess pressures by just looking at the tyres. Use a reliable pressure gauge to check your tyres, at least once a week, when they are cold. (Don't forget the spare, and remember to put the valve caps back.) Your car handbook will give the recommended pressures. It will also tell you whether the tyres need different pressures for different conditions. In general, pressures should be higher for a heavily loaded car or if you are going to drive at high speeds for long periods. Remember that it is an offence to use a car with a tyre not properly inflated.

Checking the condition of your tyres

Don't let oil or grease remain on your tyres. Anything caught in the treads—stones, glass, tacks—could work in and cause damage, so check from time to time and remove anything of this sort.

Tyres must be free from cuts and bulges. When you check your tyre walls, don't forget the inner ones (those facing each other under the car). The gripping power of a worn tyre is much reduced, particularly on wet roads. So see that all your tyres have a good depth of tread right across and all round them. (One millimetre of tread across at least three-quarters of the width and all round the tyre is the absolute minimum legal requirement.)

Uneven wear of the tread, either across or round the tyre, may be due to a mechanical defect. The wheel alignment may be wrong or the wheels out of balance, or there may be a fault in the suspension or the braking system. As soon as you see anything of this sort, have your car checked and the defect put right, and a new tyre fitted if necessary.

Replacing tyres

When you are thinking about replacing tyres, you need to distinguish between the two main types of tyre in general use— *cross-ply* and *radial-ply*. In cross-ply tyres the cords making up the tyre carcass run diagonally across it, with alternate layers at opposite angles, forming a kind of trellis. Radial-ply tyres have all the cords running at right angles across the tyre, resulting in thinner and more flexible walls. There are also differences in the way the tread of radial-ply tyres is built up, giving extra grip, especially in the wet.

A new car is normally fitted with the same type of tyre all round. If you change tyres one or two at a time, keep to the same type.

It is never safe to put radial-ply tyres at the front with cross-ply at the rear. There are no exceptions to this rule and it applies whether the car has front-wheel drive or rear-wheel drive. And don't mix cross-ply and radial-ply on the same axle. (See Fig. 59.)

Apart from its dangers, mixing radial- and cross-ply tyres obviously makes rotation of tyres (if recommended for your car) difficult if not impossible. So the answer is to keep to the same type of tyre all round. If you want to change your type of tyres, change them all if you can—all cross-ply or all radial-ply. If you have to mix types, the radial-ply tyres must go on the back wheels. Even so, the car will handle differently from the way it would with the same type of tyre all round.

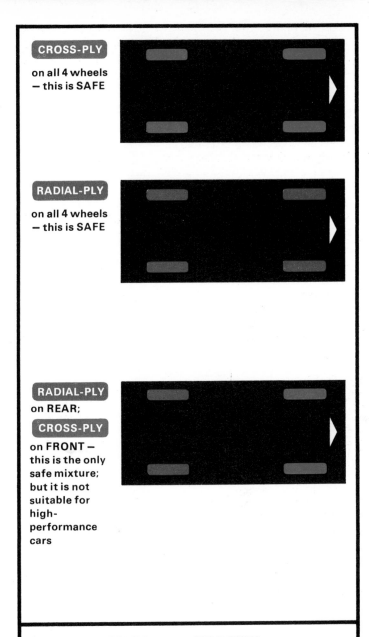

CROSS-PLY

on all 4 wheels
— this is SAFE

RADIAL-PLY

on all 4 wheels
— this is SAFE

RADIAL-PLY
on REAR;

CROSS-PLY

on FRONT —
this is the only
safe mixture;
but it is not
suitable for
high-
performance
cars

RADIALS ALL ROUND — or on REAR ONLY

NEVER put RADIALS on front only or on the same axle as
CROSS-PLY

Fig. 59
Cross- and radial-ply tyres

If you are fitting tyres of any type other than radial- or cross-ply, for example bias-belted, or thinking of mixing tyres having different characteristics, get the advice of a tyre expert.

When you replace a tubeless tyre, have a new valve fitted to the wheel. Some punctures in these tyres can be 'stopped' with rubber plugs—but this is only a temporary repair, so keep your speed down until you can get the tyre looked at thoroughly.

New tyres should be run in at reasonable speeds for the first 100 miles or so before driving at higher speeds.

If you follow this advice you should always have a good set of sound and effective tyres, which will hold the road well and help you to brake firmly. Even so, they cannot do the impossible. Your safety will still depend on your handling of the car. This is particularly true when roads are wet or icy because, however good your tyres are, they cannot grip so well in these conditions. So while on the subject of tyres and grip, let us look at what happens when you lose grip and skid.

Skidding

There are three factors in a skid; in order of importance, the driver, the vehicle and the road. Skids are more likely in some places than in others, but the part the road plays in a skid is not much more than providing somewhere for it to take place.

But skids do not just happen. They result from what a driver does with his vehicle. The driver who says 'I had a skid' (as though fate took a hand) really means 'I made a skid'. For instance, if a car is going steadily along a level road where there are no junctions, bends or traffic, there need be no skid, however slippery the road, as long as these conditions last. It is when a driver alters his *speed* or *direction* that he may skid. In other words, the risk comes when the car is being slowed down or speeded up, turned or driven uphill or downhill.

A car skids because the driver is asking more from it in braking (or acceleration) and/or steering than is possible with the amount of grip the tyres have on the road at the time.

Skids caused by braking

In Chapter 5 ('The use of brakes') we said that harsh and uncontrolled braking is one of the chief causes of skidding. Why is this? Mainly because heavy braking can lock the wheels. Brakes have their greatest stopping power when the wheels are nearly, but not quite, locked. But braking throws the weight of a car forward. The heavier the braking the more the weight is thrown to the front and the less there is on the rear wheels. The less weight on the rear wheels the less their grip and the more likely they are to lock. Then, unless braking is eased off, the front wheels lock too. The fact that the rear wheels lock first means that the car tends to swing, if not to spin.

The proof of all this is that uncontrollable skids can be produced, even with good tyres on dry roads, by drivers who do not

This tyre has a good tread—but it cannot grip so well on a wet, smooth road surface. In these circumstances your safety will depend upon how you handle the car

leave themselves enough stopping space and then brake harshly (and keep on braking) in an attempt to stop somehow. A car so treated cannot run straight for long; and as soon as it begins to swing it has only to touch something to be in danger of turning over.

Skids caused by steering

We also mentioned in Chapter 5 that when a car is turned more weight is thrown onto the front wheel on the outside of the curve. Not only is steering affected, but the lessening of weight on the back wheels can cause them to lose grip and slide.

Skids caused by acceleration

Sudden or heavy use of the accelerator—especially in the lower gears—can cause the driving wheels to spin on the road surface instead of gripping it and driving the car. Unless the accelerator pressure is very quickly eased off, the car could go into a skid because of this wheelspin.

Skids caused by braking and steering

To combine two possible methods of producing a skid—wrong braking and wrong steering—is to ask for real trouble. If your tyres are only just gripping while you are cornering and you then start to brake (or if they are only just gripping while you are braking and you then start to corner), locked wheels and a skid are inevitable. You can't expect your tyres to do the impossible.

The answer to all this is simple—and has already been mentioned. Give yourself plenty of room to work in. The other point

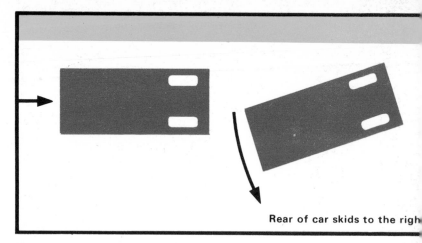

Rear of car skids to the righ[t]

Fig. 60
Steering 'into' a rear-wheel skid

to remember is that when roads are wet or icy your tyres have less grip to start with. So you must brake, steer and accelerate very much more gently in these conditions because your 'grip margin' is that much smaller. The best way to give yourself time to do this is to keep your speed down. We go into these points in more detail later in the chapter.

Avoiding skids

However skilful you are, the result of skidding must, in today's traffic, be largely a matter of pure chance. There is no system of skid control so effective as driving in a way that will avoid them. Drivers not only make skids but, having made them, can make them much worse. Here is some advice on how to avoid skids:

1 *On very slippery surfaces your stopping distance can be as much as ten times longer than on a dry road*

2 Be on the look-out for signs of slippery roads. Any wet road should be regarded as being slippery. Rain, ice and packed snow are obvious causes of slippery roads, but they are not the only ones. Frost can linger in shaded places well on into the day; wet mud can be almost as slippery as ice at any time of the year. Loose surfaces and wet leaves on the road are other danger signs. (See 'Anticipation' in Chapter 5 and 'Weather and vision' on page 166)

3 When you suspect that the road is slippery, keep your speed down. Your brakes will not get you out of trouble when tyre grip is poor. *They are far more likely to get you into it.* It helps to use engine braking by changing down in good time, but be very careful with the accelerator and clutch—misused, they can cause skids too. (See 'Wet roads', 'Braking on snow

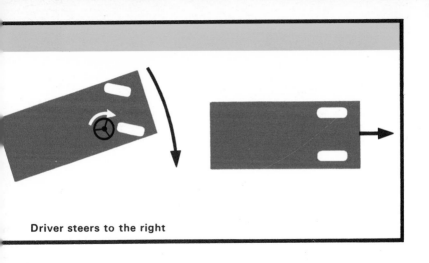

Driver steers to the right

and ice' and 'Climbing hills on snow and ice' later in this chapter)

4 Keeping your car in good condition will help to avoid skids. Brakes that snatch or pull unevenly are dangerous in slippery conditions. An accelerator pedal linkage which is jerky can cause wheel spin

Dealing with skids

If you should find yourself in a skid while braking, the first thing to do is to *release the brake pedal altogether*. This is more easily said than done, because the natural tendency is to try to stop the car by using the brake still more. Drivers often 'freeze' with the right foot hard down on the brake and hang on, all through a skid, with the wheels locked. This only makes matters worse. In any skid, keep off the brakes.

A skid may be no more than a slight slide of the rear of the car, which can be felt rather than seen. This can be corrected by a slight movement of the steering wheel in the same direction as the skid (and perhaps by easing off the accelerator as well) to bring the front and back wheels into line again.

If the skid has developed beyond the stage of a slight slide, easing off the accelerator is more important, and more definite steering into the skid is needed. This means that if the *rear* of your car is going *left* you should *steer* to the *left* to bring the front wheels into line with the rear ones. If the *rear* of your car is going to the *right*, *steer* to the *right* (see Fig. 60). But beware of over-correction by too much steering movement of the front wheels, which will lead to another skid in the opposite direction. If the front wheels seem to be sliding instead of, or as well as, the back ones, release the accelerator and don't try to steer the car until they regain some of their grip. With a front-wheel drive car, too much power can produce a front-wheel skid, but easing the accelerator will usually help to correct this.

Burst tyres (blow-outs)

The main danger of a tyre bursting is that the car will swerve or weave. This risk is increased if the brakes are applied, so use them as little as possible—and certainly avoid heavy braking. Hold the steering wheel very firmly to check any swerving—but beware of over-correction. The aim should be to let the car roll to a safe stopping place.

Weather hazards

Weather hazards can range from no more than having to put a vizor down against the sun to being completely stuck in a snowdrift. Having your car, and its equipment, in good condition and properly adjusted can be more than half the battle. In bad weather it is even more important that your tyres should be sound, have good treads and be properly inflated, because their grip on the road will be less and you cannot afford to lose any more of it by having tyres below par. Similarly, the effect of brakes badly adjusted or out of balance will be worse because the tyres have less grip. This could lead to the car pulling to one side when braked, or to braking in jerks ('snatching and grabbing').

As far as your driving is concerned, weather has to be reckoned with just as much as the amount of traffic. Even on a short journey the weather may vary so much that constant alertness is needed. Daytime mist, for example, may be fairly easy to deal with if the sun is out overhead so that there is a good background of light. But on the other side of the hill the same mist can be freezing on your windscreen in a matter of seconds.

Even the wind can be a hazard. This is dealt with in some detail under 'Weather on motorways', page 180; but windy weather can cause difficulty—and danger—on any road, so be ready for its effect on the handling of your vehicle.

Common sense gives—or should do—the most important of all weather rules. On wet or icy roads, or in fog, keep your speed well down. The worse the conditions the slower your speed, is a good summary, but it is only the beginning of the story of bad weather driving. The rest of this chapter fills in the detail of the ways in which you can, whatever the weather, still keep your grip.

Weather and vision

The biggest single danger to any driver is being unable to see properly. One of the ways in which weather often makes vision poor is by causing the inside glass of your car, including the mirror, to mist up. Misting has many causes, from winter fog to a sudden shower on a summer day. You can do a lot to overcome misting by keeping the inside glass clean, by wiping it dry before you start out, and by making the best use of your demister and any other means of ventilation, including open windows.

There are many anti-mist (and anti-frost) accessories available —liquid for the glass, prepared cloths, panels for double glazing the back window, and electrically heated glass. Best of all is plenty of warm dry air. You won't have this when you start up from cold, so experiment to find out what suits your particular car. Whatever you use, it is sensible to keep a piece of clean dry wash leather or suitable cloth handy so that you can dry the inside of the windscreen when necessary. If the inside of the rear and side windows need wiping, get your passengers to do it. If you haven't any passengers, stop and do it yourself. When it is very cold the outside of the glass may ice up. This can, and should, mean delay until the ice or frost has been melted off.

Study your car handbook so that you know how to get the very best out of any ventilating and heating system fitted. Whatever you do, don't drive unless you can see properly all round. Treat any other cars you see which are misted up as special hazards.

Rain and vision

Apart from misting up the windows inside the car, rain can cause loss of vision by obscuring the outside of the screen and windows. The cleaner you keep the glass of your car, the sooner the wipers will be able to clear the outside of the screen, and the less you will be hampered by wet and dirty side and rear windows. (Keep the washer bottle topped up.) At higher speeds some windscreen wiper blades lose their pressure on the windscreen, or even lift off, and this affects vision very severely. In dirty weather take every chance to clean your lamps and indicators.

When heavy rain and spray cut visibility use your headlights so that other road users can see you.

Wet roads

When roads are wet, braking distances increase because tyre grip is reduced. Give yourself much more room for slowing down and stopping. Water on the road makes a slippery film, especially after a spell of dry weather.

Your allowance for braking distance when the road is wet should be *at least doubled*. Be on the look-out for differences in road surfaces which may reduce the grip of your tyres still more. The smoother your tyres the greater the increase in braking distance on a wet road.

Surface water

Rain can be so heavy that it forms a thin sheet of water all over the road. Even good tyres cannot grip through this. The surface water can then build up under the tyres so that your car is just sliding forwards, not in contact with the road at all. This is called aquaplaning. In this situation you would have no control at all

Fog is one of the most dangerous weather conditions a driver has to face. An accident to one vehicle may so quickly involve many others. The first and best precaution in mist or fog is to slow down (*Photographic material courtesy of Uniroyal Limited*)

over steering or braking. The higher your speed on a road as wet as this, the more likely you are to aquaplane. This just reinforces the advice—slow down in the wet.

Quite apart from keeping proper control on wet roads, there is another reason for slowing down which marks the good and considerate driver. Driving too fast through pools of water can drench pedestrians and also smother other people's windscreens, if not your own. Water thrown up under your car can affect your brakes and, spread around under the bonnet, it can stop the engine. There is no profit in plunging through puddles.

Above, top
Don't let mist or fog on your windscreen make it more difficult for you to see.
Above, lower
Use your windscreen wipers.

Floods

Don't rush things. Stop and find out how deep the water is. If it is not too deep and you decide to drive through, notice if there is a camber on the road so that you can keep to the shallowest part of the water. Drive through in first gear as slowly as you can, but keep the engine speed high and steady. Slip the clutch to keep the engine speed up but the actual speed of the car down. You will have to strike a balance. If the engine speed is too low you will stall. If you go too fast you may build up too much of a wave and water will get over the engine.

Use headlights in daytime mist or fog. The side lights on the overtaking car show up only when the outline of the vehicle itself can be seen

As soon as you have driven through a stretch of flooded road, try your brakes. You will probably find that they are of little use because they need drying out. You can do this by driving very slowly with your left foot pressing lightly on the brake pedal. Make sure your brakes are working properly again before going back to normal speeds.

Fords

Watch out for a depth gauge; in winter especially there can be quite a depth of water. Otherwise, use the same technique as you would for a flood. At the far side there may be a sign reminding you to try your brakes; in any case remember for yourself to try them out, and dry them out if necessary.

Fog

Fog is not only frustrating but is also one of the most dangerous weather conditions a driver has to face, because an accident to one vehicle can so quickly involve many others. The thickness of fog can change quickly and you can find yourself in dense fog very suddenly. Because fog reduces a driver's ability to anticipate and react to changes of situation ahead, the first thing you must do is to reduce speed. *You must be able to stop well within the distance you can see to be clear.* The second is to make sure that none of the fog is being created or carried on your own screen, inside or out. Use the demister and windscreen wipers to take care of that —and keep them going.

Lights in fog

In daylight, use headlights when it is misty or foggy; they can be seen from a far greater distance. Side lights may not be seen by other drivers or pedestrians until your car is itself visible— which is too late. Even headlights on full beam will not usually dazzle or inconvenience other drivers in daytime mist or fog. *At dusk*, and at other times when overhead daylight is poor, use dipped beams.

In darkness you may have to depend entirely on fog lamps, but foggy or misty conditions can change quickly, so do not settle down to fog lamps only. You may find that over some stretches dipped beams will give a better view ahead. Adapt your choice of lights as conditions vary.

Following another vehicle in fog

Leave yourself plenty of room for stopping. There may be something ahead *which you cannot possibly see*, which will mean an emergency stop for the vehicle in front. Space is vital because you will first have to see and recognise that the vehicle ahead is stopping or has stopped, and then you still have your thinking and braking distances to allow for. Make up your own mind about a safe speed—and keep to it. Don't be tempted to keep up with the vehicle in front just for the sake of it. 'Follow my leader' can be a dangerous game in fog.

Another pitfall is that when you are driving behind another vehicle the fog will seem less thick than it really is, because some of it will be displaced by the other vehicle. Resist the urge to overtake, which is highly dangerous in fog. If you start to overtake, you may find that visibility ahead is much worse than you think.

Finally, another point about lights when you are following a vehicle. Don't use lights which shine so far forward that they cast a shadow of the vehicle ahead on the fog in front of it. This can make things very difficult for its driver.

Junctions in fog

Turning at a junction in fog, especially to the right, needs a lot of care. Lower your windows so that you can hear, start the indicators well beforehand and make the greatest possible use of your car lights. If you have to wait for other vehicles to pass before you can turn, keep your foot on the brake pedal so that your stop lights are on as an extra warning to following traffic. Use the horn and listen for possible answers. Don't turn until you have made as sure as you can that it is safe.

Road markings in fog

A fog lamp may pick out reflective studs (cat's-eyes) well, but generally it is not so easy to recognise other road markings in fog. Local knowledge, gained from earlier observation, particularly of edge of carriageway or similar markings, will help you tremendously. When you can see lane lines or studs, try to keep centrally between them. But don't mix up lane lines and centre lines. Driving right up to the centre line could put you too close to someone coming the other way and doing the same thing. (Details of how line markings vary are given on page 100 in Chapter 8.)

Parking in fog

Never park on a road in fog. Find an off-street parking place. If your vehicle breaks down, or if you have to leave it for any reason, get it off the road if you possibly can. If you can't do this, never leave it without warning lights of some kind—or on the 'wrong' side of the road.

Snow and ice

Falling snow, like rain, can have varying effects on driving. Sometimes it melts on the windscreen or doesn't lie on the road at all. At other times traffic churns it up and keeps it slushy, especially in the daytime on busy roads, or if the road has been gritted or salted.

Except in heavy snow-storms, falling or freshly fallen snow does not usually cause much difficulty, provided you are sensible and remember four points. First, once again, that you need to increase the gap between you and the vehicle in front. Second, that sticky snow can pack behind the front wheels or round brake linkages under the car and so affect steering and braking. So test your brakes, very gently, from time to time. Third, that your wipers, even when helped by the heater, may not be able to sweep a lot of snow clear, and you may have to stop and clear the windscreen by hand. Fourth, that you may be getting packed snow on your lamp and indicator glasses. This will need clearing away, especially if you are driving at night.

Always clear your rear window before you start driving, and then keep it clear.

Overnight freezing of already packed-down snow usually results in an icy surface, particularly on less well-used roads. Driving on ice has been compared with walking on eggs. Certainly this gives the right idea. Every control—brakes, accelerator, steering, clutch and gears—must be used very delicately. Roads are often more slippery when it is just beginning to freeze (or thaw) and there is both ice and water on them. Another danger is glazed frost, caused by rain freezing on roads as it falls. You will not be able to see this 'black ice' on a wet road. The first warning of it may be that the steering feels light. So when there is any risk of this, keep your speed well down.

Braking on snow and ice

Anything except the most gentle braking will lock the wheels on ice. If your front wheels lock you cannot steer the car, and if you can't steer you can't keep out of trouble.

Braking distances on ice can easily be *ten times* as much as normal. Downhill braking, especially to a stop, calls for careful control of speed both before you reach the hill and while you are on it. Get into a lower gear earlier than usual, allow your speed to drop and, if necessary, use the brake pedal, gently and early, to keep your speed down to what you can control.

Corners and bends on snow and ice

Your front wheels are even more likely to lock if you brake while you are turning. Time your driving so that you do not have to touch the brakes at all *on the corner*. Take corners at a steady speed, in as high a gear as you reasonably can.

Be delicate with the accelerator pedal and leave the clutch alone as much as you can. Steer smoothly; sudden movements of the steering wheel must be avoided at all costs. This also applies to straightening up after the turn, which calls for just as much delicacy in handling the controls.

Starting off on snow

If you have wheelspin when trying to start off in deep snow, don't go on racing the engine. This will only dig the wheel or wheels in deeper. Try moving your car slightly backwards and then forwards to get out of the rut. Use the highest gear you can for the conditions.

Climbing hills on snow and ice

Although speed generally must be kept down on slippery roads, the loss of momentum going uphill may mean that you won't get up at all. Trying to regain lost speed may cause such severe wheelspin that you lose control. If you have to stop, it may be very difficult to start again. Here again, leave a good gap behind the vehicle in front. Then, if it stops on the hill you will have at least a chance to keep going while it re-starts or, possibly, to pass it. Traffic that is well spaced out helps to avoid queues and hold-ups on slippery roads.

Use the highest gear you reasonably can. This gives the least increase in speed of the driving wheels for any given movement of the accelerator pedal, and reduces the chance of wheelspin. If some wheelspin is unavoidable, the less you have of it the better. Don't try to rush a hill with the idea of changing down on the way up. Choose the best gear for the whole climb and make it in that gear. Changing gear on the way up is not easy. Even for the best driver, it needs very delicate footwork to avoid wheelspin and loss of speed.

Other vehicles on snow and ice

No driver wants to see a vehicle coming towards him that is obviously out of control. But it does happen. In some situations there may not be much you can do about it. Your main thought will naturally be to get out of the way, either by steering or braking. But as we have seen, both are dangerous in icy conditions. Make use of engine braking if there is time and, if you must use the brake pedal, do it as gently as you can. But whatever you do, don't make matters worse by trying to steer and brake at the same time.

Summary

1

The need for good tyres; regular checks; saving wear and tear

2

Radial-ply and cross-ply tyres; the dangers of mixing them

3

Skids—how they are caused and how to avoid them; correcting skids

4

Driving in bad weather; leaving a bigger gap and driving more slowly on wet or icy roads

5

Floods and fords; how to deal with them

6

Driving in fog; speed and spacing; use of lights

7

Snow and ice—the main problems

14 Motorway driving

There are no ordinary junctions, sharp bends, roundabouts, steep hills or traffic lights on motorways. Traffic is less mixed than on other roads; it is all one-way and the slowest vehicles are excluded. Traffic can therefore safely travel faster over longer distances, but this makes lane discipline even more important than on ordinary roads.

The driver on a motorway

What about the driver in all this? As with driving on any road, you need to be fit. It is particularly unwise to go on to a motorway if you are at all below par. This is not only because alertness is so important for motorway driving, but because parking is prohibited and if you need to rest you may have to go quite a long way before you get to an exit point or a service area where you can stop.

The higher speeds on motorways mean that you need more time for almost every driving action. In other words, you need to give yourself bigger margins than on ordinary roads; bigger margins of roadworthiness and of space between your car and the one in front. This chapter describes why these bigger margins are so important.

Your vehicle on a motorway

Before using a motorway make quite sure that your vehicle is in good order, especially the tyres. See that your tyre pressures are high enough. Instruments and warning lights are important too, because higher speeds over long distances increase the risk of mechanical failure. Check that you have plenty of petrol, oil and water. Motorway speeds use them up faster and to run out of any of them can be dangerous, inconvenient and costly.

Joining a motorway: The slip road leads into an acceleration lane. Watch the traffic on the motorway and adjust your speed so that you can join the left-hand lane in a suitable gap

Don't flog your car. Choose a steady speed (within the speed limits) which suits you and your vehicle and the weather conditions.

Getting on to a motorway

Motorways usually start at a roundabout, unless a main road becomes a motorway. Elsewhere you will get on to them by a slip road which leads into an acceleration lane. This lane is an extra piece of road from which you can see, and adjust to, the motorway traffic and its speed before you become part of it. *You must give way to traffic already on the motorway, taking your place only when there is a suitable gap in the left-hand lane.* Once you have joined the motorway stay in the left-hand lane until you have had time to judge and get used to the speeds at which the traffic is moving.

Seeing on a motorway

Don't put unnecessary difficulties in the way of being able to see properly. Start out with clean mirrors, screen and windows. Use the washers, wipers and demisters freely whenever necessary. Keep your eyes moving so that you can see things, near and far, to the front and rear. Use your mirror even sooner than you would on an ordinary road and check it more often, because the higher motorway speeds are more difficult to judge and situations develop very quickly. Any increase in the number of vehicles you can see ahead may mean that traffic is slowing down for some reason—a warning to you to reduce speed until you are sure just what is happening.

Being seen on a motorway

Your car is often visible to other drivers on a motorway much earlier than it would be on an ordinary road. It needs to be, because of the higher speeds. If the daylight is at all poor use your side and rear lights at least. If it is hazy or misty in daytime use your headlights.

Ventilation

Driving on a motorway can get monotonous and cause drowsiness. Avoid this by making full use of whatever ventilation system you have. Keep the car warm but well aired. If you still feel drowsy keep a window open until you can get to a service area. There, open all the windows. Better still, get out into the air for a while.

Spacing

A gap of at least one yard for each mph of your speed is an absolute minimum. If the road is wet or icy the gap should be much longer. In the worst weather conditions you could need up to ten times the stopping distance that you do for a dry road.

Headlamp flashing

The higher noise level on motorways, particularly in wet weather, may prevent other drivers from hearing your horn. Flashing your headlamps is usually a better warning of your presence when one is necessary. By the same token, be alert for such a warning yourself.

Changing lanes on a motorway

Change lanes only when there is need. Keep in the middle of the lane you are using and don't let your car wander from side to side or into another lane.

When you do need to change lanes use the *mirror—signal—manoeuvre* routine, remembering how quickly vehicles may come up behind you. This routine is vital for motorway safety. Start it much earlier than on an ordinary road so that your indicators are seen well before you start your move. This should tell all who can see them that a shift in the traffic pattern is coming, even though they may not be able to see why, and give them time to prepare for it.

Two-lane discipline

On a two-lane motorway the normal driving position is in the left-hand lane. The right-hand (offside) lane is for overtaking.

Three-lane discipline

The normal driving rule still applies—well to the left; that is, in the left-hand lane. But if there are so many slower moving vehicles in that lane that you would be moving in and out repeatedly, you may stay in the middle lane. The right-hand (offside) lane is for overtaking; it is *not* 'the fast lane'. Don't stay in it any longer than is needed to move out, overtake and then move in again, all with a good safety margin.

If you are towing a caravan or any other kind of trailer, or driving a heavy goods vehicle, you must not use the right-hand lane. This restriction does not apply in exceptional circumstances such as the temporary closing of one or more of the other lanes.

Braking

Because of the high speeds on motorways any braking must be unhurried, progressive and properly spread out. The need to spread your braking adds point to the importance of proper spacing, which has already been mentioned. And *mirror* first—every time.

Overtaking

This is almost entirely a matter of proper spacing and good margins. The *position—speed—look* routine is the first thing to think about. The correct *position* is well back from the vehicle you are going to overtake, so that you can move out on a smooth, easy course when you are ready. No sudden lurch to the right.

Next, *speed*: are you going fast enough, or can you accelerate enough, to overtake without balking anything coming up faster behind you? Then, *look*—ahead to make sure there is nothing to prevent you from overtaking safely (a lane closed for repairs, for example) and behind you.

Mirror checks are vital on a motorway; and remember that vehicles may be coming up from behind much faster than you think. Next, *signal*—well before you start to move out. (We have all seen drivers who start their signalling dangerously late, when they are already the best part of the way into their new lane.) After a final mirror check, pull out smoothly into your overtaking lane, get past and back into the left as soon as you can, taking care not to move in too soon in front of the vehicle you have passed. Be particularly careful to see that indicator signals are cancelled after you have completed your lane changes. The comparatively slight movements of the steering wheel may not be enough to work a self-cancelling device.

Normally you should never overtake on the left. But where the traffic is moving in queues, and the traffic queue on the right is going more slowly than you are, you may maintain the speed of the traffic in your own lane and so pass on the left.

Changes in traffic conditions

In deciding when to carry out a manœuvre, and how much margin to leave, remember that traffic conditions can vary on motorways as much as on any other road. Some stretches attract considerable

Leaving a motorway: The deceleration lane and slip road at a motorway exit give you time and space to begin to adjust to the lower speeds on an ordinary road.

rush hour traffic where they run near towns. Other stretches may have no particular rush hours. Differences of this sort are likely to have much more effect on two-lane motorways.

Motorway interchanges

Where motorways join or separate, your route may require you to change lanes. Sometimes more than one lane change will be necessary. Pay attention to the overhead direction signs and move into the correct lane in good time.

Leaving a motorway

If you are not going to the end of the motorway you leave it by moving left from the left-hand lane into a deceleration lane (extra strip) which takes you on to the exit road.

Don't rush this in any way. Use your mirror, and signal in good time. There are plenty of signs to help you with your timing so that you can give yourself the necessary margins. One mile before the exit (unless, unusually, there are exits very close together) you will see a sign for the junction with road numbers. At half a mile another sign with place names as well. Farther on there will be 'count-down' markers at 300 yards, 200 yards and finally 100 yards before the beginning of the deceleration lane. Use this succession of signs and markers to spread your use of mirror and indicators, your change of lane and speed—and if necessary your braking. This will leave a margin all round for yourself and the other drivers affected by your action.

Unless you are already in the left-hand lane, the first step is to get into that lane. On a three-lane motorway this may mean more than one lane change. If so, you must follow the *mirror—signal—manœuvre* routine for *each one*. Don't move to the left more than one lane at a time, and don't cut straight across into the deceleration lane. Move into the deceleration lane so that you can slow down before you join the exit road. If you miss your turn-off point you must carry on until you reach the next one. Never reverse, turn in the road or cross the central reservation.

There are END OF MOTORWAY signs at all exits from these roads. Remember that these also mean that the road you are joining is subject to different rules, so watch for any signs which tell you what these are—speed limits, dual carriageway or two-way traffic and so on.

Speed when leaving a motorway

After some miles of driving on a motorway your judgment of your own speed will almost certainly be affected. Nearly everyone underestimates—40 or 45 mph may seem more like 20. Use your speedometer, especially when you get on the exit road from the motorway, and until you have had time to readjust to the slower speeds on ordinary roads. This readjustment takes several minutes.

Weather on motorways

All that was said in Chapter 13 about driving in poor weather conditions applies even more strongly on motorways. For instance, wet weather can make visibility much worse because vehicles (especially big ones) travelling at higher speeds throw up more spray, particularly on exposed stretches.

Never drive at fine-weather speeds when conditions are poor. Use side lights in the daytime and headlights if necessary. Keep your speed down and leave much longer gaps; you need a bigger margin because braking distances are far longer on wet roads. If there is a danger of frost or ice, notice the feel of your steering. Any lightness is a danger sign. A *very* gentle touch on your brakes occasionally, to see how they respond, is a sensible precaution.

Cross-winds are another motorway hazard. They may affect your steering much more than on ordinary roads. If the wind is coming from your left, be especially careful when passing a large vehicle. A sudden gust as you come out from the shelter of the vehicle could make your car swerve to the right. Wind effects are also increased as you come out of the shelter of bridges or high embankments.

When there is a fog on a motorway the only safe rule is that *you must be able to stop well within the distance you can see to be clear.* Fog affects not only visibility but also judgment of speed and distance so, once again, *reduce speed.* Even if other drivers are ignoring this elementary safety rule, there is no reason why you should. Unless the fog is so thick that visibility restricts you to an absolute crawl, you can easily find yourself speeding up without realising it, so glance at your speedometer occasionally.

Motorway signals

There are signal lights on motorways to warn you of such dangers ahead as accidents, fog or the risk of slippery roads. The earlier type of warning, at one-mile intervals, consists of two amber lights, one above the other, which flash alternately to convey the general message—'Danger ahead—slow down to 30 mph or less'. These are being replaced by later types. On rural (country) motorways, these newer signals, which are at two-mile intervals, have a double pair of amber lights flashing alternately and an illuminated symbol giving advised maximum speeds or information about closed lanes. On urban (town) motorways these new signals are fixed overhead at shorter intervals. They have red flashing lights to indicate STOP (for closed lanes), or flashing amber lights with illuminated symbols to show the lane to be taken, or the advised maximum speed (see Fig. 61).

Some motorways may have other special signals—warning of high winds on the Severn Bridge, for example. Whichever type of signal is in use:

STOP if you see flashing red lights

SLOW DOWN if you see flashing amber lights—to the advised speed, or follow the course shown

If you do not have to stop, be ready, when you see the danger itself, to slow down still more; to a crawl if necessary

Look out for police notices and diversion signs

Remember that fog can drift rapidly and is often patchy. Even if it seems to be clearing there can be a sudden thick patch ahead

If you can see that you need to slow down or stop, start to do so much sooner than usual and treat all controls gently, especially the brakes

Where the earlier-type signals are flashing, keep below 30 mph until you are sure that it is safe to go faster again. Where figures are shown on the signals, do not exceed this advised maximum speed

Motorway signals above lanes

Earlier type signals

The flashing amber lights tell you that an advised maximum speed of 30 m.p.h. is in operation, and warn of danger ahead (such as accident, fog or risk of skidding)

Motorway signals beside the carriageway

At entrances

These signals may have red as well as amber lights. If flashing amber lights change to flashing red lights YOU MUST STOP AT THE SIGNAL

On central reserva

This signal is showing advised maximum spee 20 m.p.h. (other speed may be shown)

Fig. 61

...hen amber lights flash above your lane, one of these symbols will tell you...

...move to the
...e on your left

...move to the
lane on your right

...leave motorway
at the next exit

...the advised
maximum speed
(other speeds
may be shown)

...he flashing amber lights change to flashing
...lights YOU MUST STOP AT THE SIGNAL

This symbol
(which appears
without flashing
lights) tells you
that the lane is clear

...en amber lights flash you will see an advised maximum speed
...one of the following symbols which will tell you...

...ight-hand lane
...sed

...left-hand and
middle lanes
closed

...right-hand and
middle lanes
closed

...eft-hand lane
...ed

...left-hand lane
closed

...right-hand lane
closed

This symbol
(which appears
without flashing
lights) tells you
that the road is
clear

183

Fig. 62
Emergency telephone

Fig. 63
Motorway junction sign
with inset junction number

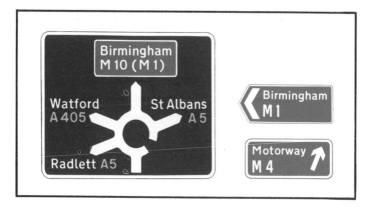

Fig. 64
Motorway signs

Stops on motorways

Apart from the flashing red lights just mentioned, you may also be signalled to stop by the police or by an emergency traffic sign. Otherwise, you are allowed to stop on the carriageway only if by doing so you will prevent or avoid an accident. If you do have to stop on the carriageway, and if your vehicle is equipped so that you can switch on all the direction indicators to flash together, do so as a warning signal.

The hard shoulder at the side of the motorway is for use only in emergency—not for sightseeing stops, picnics or taking a rest. If you break down, get your vehicle on to the hard shoulder as soon as you can. If the breakdown affects your control of the car, try to keep it in a straight line while you lose speed. Avoid hard braking if at all possible, and aim at steering gently on to the hard shoulder. When you get there don't open the offside doors. Warn your passengers of the danger of passing vehicles, and keep children and animals off the carriageway—in the car if possible.

Emergency telephones

There are emergency telephones connected to a police control point on most stretches of motorway, usually at one-mile intervals. If you need a telephone, look at the marker posts along the hard shoulder—they are usually 110 yards apart—for a telephone symbol with an arrow (see Fig. 62). This will show you the way to the nearest telephone.

Parking

The only parking places along a motorway are the specially provided service areas. When you go into a service area be very careful about your speed. Getting down to car park speeds will seem like crawling after motorway speeds. Be as careful about your passengers, especially children and animals, as you would on the hard shoulder. Other drivers will be coming very close after driving at motorway speeds and spacing. Parts of the service area are carriageways, so when you get out of your car turn yourself into a careful pedestrian and look after children and animals.

The only exit from a service area is back on to the motorway. The joining procedure is the same as at any other slip road and acceleration lane.

Motorway signs

The signs which direct you from ordinary roads to motorways have white letters and figures on a blue panel, usually with a white border. You may see these blue panels either as separate signs or included in larger signs of various colours.

The map-type advance direction signs and count-down markers on the motorways themselves have already been mentioned. Other advance direction signs give information about service areas. All advance direction signs on motorways are very much larger than those on ordinary roads so that you can read them from a greater distance—a constant and practical reminder of the need for good margins for error (see Figs. 63 and 64).

You will notice from Fig. 63 that each motorway junction has an identifying number. These numbers (which are included on up-to-date road maps) are there to help you to plan and follow your route.

Motorways at night

The next chapter deals with driving at night, wherever you are. Nearly all of it applies to motorway driving, but take special note of 'Your eyes at night' on page 187. The point about giving your eyes time to begin to adapt to darkness is an important one if you have just come out of a well-lit service area.

Here are some special points about motorways at night:

1 Speeds and distances are more deceptive than on ordinary roads

2 Dazzle can still be a problem for oncoming drivers, especially if you are on a long left-hand bend. Use dipped beams if dazzle is likely

3 If you are dazzled and have to slow down, remember the traffic behind—don't brake too suddenly

4 Judging the speed and judging the distance of other vehicles are both more difficult *on a motorway and at night*. This means that changing lanes, whether to pass other drivers or to leave the motorway, needs special care. Use your indicators sooner—that is, for longer periods. If you have any doubt at all about the safety of a particular manœuvre, don't make it

Summary

1

Making sure that you and your vehicle are in good shape

2

Joining a motorway

3

Seeing and being seen

4

The importance of good spacing and early signalling

5

Lane discipline and overtaking

6

Leaving a motorway; checking your speed

7

Bad weather driving on motorways

8

Emergency warning signals, stops and telephones

9

Special points about night driving on motorways

15

Night driving

Even in perfect weather and with good headlights properly adjusted, you cannot see as far or as much at night as you can in daylight. So you cannot possibly know as much about what is ahead of you and around you. The night-time need is therefore for even more alertness and a realisation that you cannot safely drive as fast as you would do in daytime.

So far as driving is concerned, the word 'night' includes the periods of dusk and dawn—not just the hours between official lighting-up and switching-off times. Towards dusk it may well be wise to put your lights on before lighting-up time, even if it is not legally necessary. Be guided by the conditions. It is not a bad thing to be the first to switch on (even if this does produce reproachful switchings on and off by other drivers who seem to think you have put your lights on by mistake). In the mornings the opposite applies. Don't switch off until you are sure that other drivers can see you and that you will be just as safe without lights. Even the colour of the car comes into this. If yours is dark— navy blue, brown, grey and so on—switch on earlier and switch off later.

Apart from being able to see your car more easily, other drivers will be able to tell, from seeing your lights, *which way* you are going—very important in conditions of changing light.

Your eyes at night

The need to have your eyesight checked regularly was mentioned in Chapter 5. Night driving in particular may show a need for a check. Can you really see as well as you would like to? Could your eyes be partly to blame? If you have doubts, this is the time to get a check.

On dark nights you may have no more visibility than this on an unlit road. Under these conditions the rule is: if you cannot stop well within the range of your lights you are going too fast

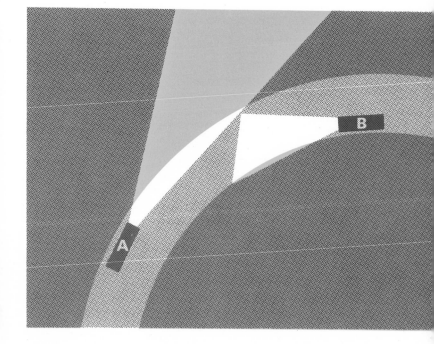

Fig. 65

Headlights on bends

Driver A, on a right-hand bend, is about to dip

Driver B, on a left-hand bend, needs to dip much earlier

Even if your sight is perfect your eyes will take some time to adapt to darkness. Don't come out of a brightly lit building and drive off straightaway. Give your eyes time to begin to adjust; closing them for a moment or two helps. Wait at least a minute or two before you start driving. You can fill in the time usefully by wiping your lights, windscreen, mirror and so on, and your spectacles if you wear them. The windscreen is particularly important—a clean screen cuts down dazzle.

Your vehicle lights

At night vehicle lights replace most of the many daylight sources of information about what is ahead. They also tell other road users about your movements. Your safety therefore depends on them, so keep them in proper order and use them sensibly and with consideration for other people. Get the most out of them by such simple precautions as a wipe over after driving on wet roads. Check them before any long journey.

The adjustment and setting of headlights is important and these too should be checked periodically. Whenever a lighting fault occurs get it put right straightaway—a new bulb or whatever it is. If you don't you will be a danger to yourself and others.

Speed at night

Speed limits apart, the general rule about never driving so fast that you cannot stop well within the distance you can see to be clear means, at night, 'within your lights'. If you cannot stop well within the range of your own lights (or of other available lighting) you are going too fast. Try it out in a suitable place. Look for an object which is just within the range of your lights and then see if you can stop by the time you get to it. This test may give you something of a shock if you try it with *dipped* headlights on an unlighted road. It will certainly show how much easier it is to pick out white or light coloured objects than darker ones. It will also show the value of a good look ahead before you dip your headlights for a driver coming towards you.

Auxiliary driving lamps can help you pick out pedestrians or cyclists when you are on dipped beams. But it is most important for such lamps to be properly aimed—well to the left and only just high enough to give you a slightly earlier view, without dazzling oncoming drivers.

Meeting other vehicles at night

The lights of another vehicle usually tell you its direction of travel. They may tell you very little about its speed. Lights coming towards you should raise a number of questions in your mind. These will vary with the sort of road you are on—but here are some of the chief ones:

1 How far away is he—and how fast is he coming?

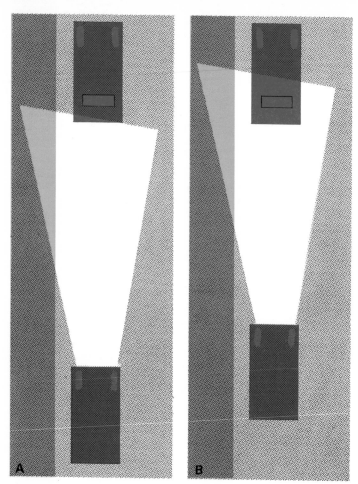

Fig. 66
Following on dipped headlights

Correct (A)
(provided that your speed is low enough)

Wrong (B)
—front driver is dazzled through his rear window

2 Is this the sort of road where I should slow down while we pass each other?

3 How soon should I dip?

4 How far ahead can I see before I dip?

5 Before I dip, is there anything in the way on my side of the road—stationary vehicles, cyclists, pedestrians?

On roads where headlights on full beam are necessary, dip soon enough to help oncoming drivers and riders, but not too soon.

Dipped headlights cut down your range of vision, so dip just before you would begin to dazzle the other person. Look along your left-hand verge—not directly at oncoming headlights. Before you dip, check the road ahead as far as you can see, slowing down if necessary. This is all assuming the driver coming towards you dips too. If he doesn't, slow down or stop if necessary.

Dip earlier going round a left-hand bend, because your headlight beams will sweep across the eyes of anyone coming towards you. On a right-hand bend this doesn't happen so soon—and may not happen at all, depending on the bend (see Fig. 65).

Overtaking or following at night

The need for lower speeds at night, and the fact that you can see less than in daylight, make overtaking more difficult and less common. Less chance to overtake makes it all the more important to follow other vehicles correctly. When you come up behind another vehicle, dip your lights in good time so that the beam does not dazzle the man ahead, either through his rear window or by reflection from his mirror. If you are being overtaken, dip your headlights as soon as the other vehicle passes you.

If you drive too close, even dipped beams will dazzle the driver ahead. So the drill is: first dip, then make sure that you are far enough back for your dipped beams to fall clear of his rear window, if not of his car. In any case, you should be keeping a proper separation distance for your speed (see Fig. 66).

Where it is possible to overtake but there is oncoming traffic (on a dual carriageway, for example) don't use full beam in the face of oncoming drivers.

Built-up areas at night

Use dipped headlights in built-up areas, unless the street lighting is very good. Notice any changes in the level of street lighting and, as far as you can, adjust your own lights to suit. Watch out for pedestrians, especially those with dark clothing. They can be difficult to see, particularly where street lighting is patchy.

Junctions at night

If you are waiting at a junction, don't keep your foot on the brake pedal (except in fog). Close to, your brake lights can be dazzling, so use the handbrake. Sometimes—especially while waiting to make a right turn—you may feel that your rear indicator is dazzling the driver behind you. But don't switch it off unless you are sure that you will not mislead anyone by doing so. If you do switch off, remember to put it on again before you move off and turn.

Lights when stationary

On roads subject to a 30 mph or lower speed limit cars (and goods vehicles not exceeding 30 cwt unladen weight) may be parked without lights provided that they are not within 15 yards of a junction. You must park parallel and close to the side of the road.

Never leave your vehicle on any other road without lights—better still get it off the road altogether. With or without lights, your vehicle must not stand on the right-hand side of the road except in a one-way street.

In fog, if you cannot park your vehicle off the road, never leave it without lights.

Switch off your headlights when you stop, even if you have only stopped to set down a passenger. The fixed glare of stationary headlights can be very dazzling.

Warning instruments at night

The law says that you must not use the horn between 11.30 pm and 7 am in a built-up area (except when stationary, to avoid danger). If you need to warn other road users of your presence, flash your headlights. But remember, this is only a warning; it does not give you right of way.

Noise at night

Remember the neighbours—and children who may be asleep. Close your car doors quietly and don't rev your engine unnecessarily.

Summary

1

Your lights and your eyes

2

Speed at night

3

Meeting and overtaking other vehicles

4

Driving in built-up areas

5

Lights when stationary

6

Noise at night

16 Making things a little easier

Most jobs become easier if they are done properly, and driving is no exception. But it involves taking a little more care in the first place to save trouble later on. This chapter suggests some of the ways—many of them quite small in themselves—in which a driver can help himself and other road users. It also includes some advice for disabled drivers.

Automatic transmission

A vehicle with automatic transmission has no clutch pedal. It has instead a system that not only senses the need for changes to higher or lower gears, but makes such changes for itself. So a driver does not have to worry about the repeated decisions and movements involved in normal gear changing. This not only makes the physical job of driving that much easier but should allow a driver to give more attention to such things as earlier observation and better anticipation.

But that is not the whole story. Generally speaking, an automatic transmission changes to a higher gear as road speed rises and to a lower one as it falls. But it also takes into account the load on the engine so that (for example) it changes down, if necessary, for uphill work. But there are times when you need a low gear although your speed is constant and the engine load is light—as when you are going down a long steep hill. The automatic transmission will not necessarily choose the right gear in these situations, so you need to know how to use the particular type of controls fitted to your car to best advantage.

Selection and control of drive

Most automatics have a small selector lever, and there is usually one position or setting which corresponds to *neutral* on an ordinary gearbox. (One type, dealt with later, is an exception.) With the engine running, the selector can be moved between *driving* and *reversing* positions. These three positions are basic to most types and are often labelled D—for drive, N—for neutral, and R—for reverse, arranged in that order. Having started the engine with the selector at N (neutral), then with the lever moved to D (drive) you need only take the brakes off and press the accelerator pedal for the car to move forward. It will then continue moving, changing gears as necessary, as long as there is enough pressure on the accelerator pedal.

Because an automatic transmission is sensitive to both speed and load on the engine, heavy acceleration delays upward gear changes until the car has built up more speed. This is because hard acceleration on the flat can put much the same load on the engine as climbing a steep hill. The mechanism can only measure the load and then change gear accordingly. On one popular 1600 cc family car, automatic transmission makes the change up from first gear at any speed between something under 10 mph to just over 40 mph, according to accelerator pressure. With most automatics, the lower the speed the smoother the change.

L (lock-up or hold)

This position on the selector enables you either to keep in a low gear or to use a lower gear. In heavy slow traffic you might find that if you were using D there would be unnecessary upward and downward automatic gear changes. Using L would override the automatic mechanism and keep you in the lower gear. Similarly, if you want to change to a lower gear—for example, to go down a long steep hill—you need to use L.

Many automatic transmissions have three forward gears; the L position is usually arranged to give you, or to hold, either the middle or the lowest of these. If you select L when in second gear, it will, with most types, hold that gear only at speeds above about 5 mph. If speed drops so low that bottom gear comes in, the L position will then hold the transmission down to that gear. In other words, there will be no change back to second gear—unless, of course, you select D again.

Some automatics have only two gears, others four. The lock-up arrangements on some versions allow any gear to be selected and held; on others, any gear except top may be held.

Kick-down

Many automatics have a form of foot control called 'kick-down'. A short sharp pressure right down on the accelerator pedal, past the fully open position, causes a quick change down to the next lower gear. This ability to override the automatic mechanism, which is also possible on some automatics by 'part-throttle' operation, is very useful for quick acceleration when you need it —for overtaking, for example. To return to the higher gear again you merely ease the pressure on the accelerator pedal.

P (park)

This is a selector position, provided on many automatics for use when parking, which mechanically locks the transmission. When used, it should be selected with the car stationary and the engine stopped. (It is possible to re-start the engine with the selector lever in this position.)

Variations of selector positions

We have now looked at the five main selector positions which are found on a wide range of cars with automatic transmission. But there are many variations between different models. For example, on some cars separate markings such as D1 and D2 take the place of the D (drive) position. D2 cuts out bottom gear when moving away and gives a very smooth slow take-off in the second of the three gears—obviously very useful on slippery surfaces and in bad weather. The many other variations will be explained in the handbook for the particular car. With all automatics, it is important to study the handbook so that the fullest and safest use of all the facilities given by the particular transmission can be obtained. Some types of automatic transmission give a driver just as much opportunity for intelligent use of gears as ordinary manual transmissions.

If you haven't driven an automatic before, do your homework on the handbook. Practise and learn the selector positions by heart so that you don't have to look down at them. The makers will have put in various stops or notches to make the selector moves easy and accurate. Some points are simple: for example, if your engine stops you will need, with most types, to move the selector to neutral in order to re-start and then back to whatever setting you need for moving away. But other points may need a bit more study. As we said at the beginning of the chapter, you need to take a little trouble to start with to make the best of the advantages an automatic can give.

Before leaving the subject of selector positions, mention should be made of another type of automatic which has belt drive with pulleys that expand and contract with varying speed and load. This gives variable gear ratios with no changes as such. The lever is pushed forward for *drive* and pulled back for *reverse*. The upright position of the lever between drive and reverse corresponds to neutral. This transmission has the peculiarity that the selector lever must be in either the drive or the reverse position—and not in between them—when the engine is started. *This makes the use of the handbrake essential for safety*, especially when the choke is being used and engine revs are therefore higher.

One useful feature of this particular type is a device which can be used to put the car into the lowest available gear ratio, and to keep it there, giving a much higher degree of engine braking on very steep hills.

The importance of the handbrake

In Chapter 5 we said that, as a general rule, the handbrake should be on whenever your vehicle is stationary. With no clutch pedal, this is even more true. If the selector lever is at D, L or R (or an equivalent position) an automatic will move off under power if the accelerator is pressed—accidentally or on purpose—unless the brakes are on. If the choke is in use (and it may be an automatic choke) making the engine revs higher, an even lighter accelerator pressure can move the car away.

Another reason for using the handbrake is what is known as 'creep'. This happens if the tick-over or slow running of the engine gives enough drive to move the car. The brake is necessary to keep it still. When you drive an automatic which is new to you, check it for a tendency to excessive creep, and have the tick-over adjusted if necessary. Do the check on the level (not uphill) and remember that the effect will be even greater downhill. Don't rely on creep to hold the car on an upward slope however well it may balance with the gradient. The car could roll back without warning if the engine stopped for any reason. The safe rule is: *put your handbrake on whenever you pull up.*

Right-foot-only

The common term 'two-pedal car' rather suggests that you use one foot for each pedal. It is true that when you are manœuvring an automatic, using hardly any accelerator and only a touch on the brakes, one foot on each pedal is convenient—and safe.

But when driving along, the advantage lies entirely in using the right foot only for both accelerator and brake pedals, just as you do in a car with normal transmission. Right-foot-only develops, or helps you to maintain, anticipation; it gives all the safety factors which lie in the early release of the accelerator pedal and in early and progressive braking; it avoids the instability and wear and tear produced by braking against acceleration. There is the added advantage that there is nothing to learn or unlearn when you change from an automatic to a non-automatic, or vice versa. So tuck your left foot away.

Other points to watch

The greater need for using the handbrake when stationary has already been mentioned. There are other points that need watching, mainly because the accelerator has such a direct effect. One particular danger—apart from excessive creep—is when the tick-over is set too fast, so that the engine keeps on driving the car at what may be too high a road speed for the situation. Even

When driving an automatic, use your right foot only. It is best to tuck your left foot away

with your foot off the accelerator you could, for example, find yourself approaching a junction much too fast.

Automatics sometimes change up as you approach a corner because of reduced pressure on the accelerator. The answer is to slow down *before* the corner, then accelerate gently as you turn. As mentioned in Chapter 6, the accelerator should be used so that the engine is doing just enough work to be driving the car round the corner. This is especially important with an automatic. For very difficult corners—steep downhill ones, for example— the use of L (lock-up) will usually help but, again, go gently on the accelerator. The possible need to use lock-up selector positions for going down very steep hills has already been mentioned, but, as with low normal gears, it is important that they should be selected in good time.

Automatic systems vary a great deal in the amount of engine braking they give in some (or all) of their selector positions. Generally, the slowing effect tends to be less than it is with ordinary transmissions. Check this for yourself when you take over an automatic.

Finally, the fact that it is physically easier to drive an automatic may lead you to drive faster, perhaps unconsciously. This calls for even more anticipation and earlier observation, as well as an earlier *position—speed—look* (PSL) routine. Particularly if you are a new driver, take care that driving without clutch and gears doesn't lead you into over-confidence.

Semi-automatics and pre-selectors

In a car with semi-automatic transmission (as distinct from one with automatic transmission which itself senses the need for a gear change and makes it), the driver has to decide when a gear change is necessary and which gear to choose. The change is made simply by moving the gear lever to the position for the chosen gear. As soon as the slightest pressure is applied to the gear lever the mechanism takes over and does the necessary declutching automatically. There is no clutch pedal. When the gear lever is released the clutch is let in automatically.

'Pre-selector' transmissions, mostly found on buses and coaches, have a lever by which the driver can select gears in advance, ready for later changes. With this type, no gear change takes place until a gear-change pedal is pressed and released. A single push on this pedal sets off the process of declutching, changing into the gear already selected and then re-engaging the drive automatically. Again, this is not a clutch pedal.

Overdrive

Overdrive, fitted as an extra on some cars, can do a good deal to make things easier—perhaps more for the engine than for the driver—particularly on faster journeys. It gives an extra gear, higher than the normal top gear, in which the engine turns more slowly for the same road speed. A four-speed box can have overdrive on both third and fourth gears, giving six gears in all— one between normal third and top and one higher than top. These extra gears, which are usually engaged by no more than the flick of a switch, do not necessarily make the car go faster, but they can save wear and tear (even though some acceleration may be lost).

The disabled driver

The need for easy transport encourages many disabled people to make remarkable efforts; and those who drove before they became handicapped are often spurred on to learn new skills in order to master vehicles and drive them safely. Disabilities can vary so much and call for so many different sorts of adaptations to the controls that it is not possible to mention them all here in detail. But we do describe some of the possibilities in fairly general terms.

Two-pedal cars

Automatic transmissions can be a great help to drivers with physical handicaps, simply because there is less work for feet and hands to do. Using the good foot for both accelerator and brake pedal can put the driver with a leg or foot disability on almost equal terms with the driver who has the use of both feet. An arm too weak to work normal gear levers may be quite capable of using small and easily moved selector levers, as well as doing its share of steering. Semi-automatics reduce footwork too, and disabled drivers may find the special gear levers easier to use when there is no clutch to be operated as well.

Adapted cars

Apart from the help which automatic transmissions can give disabled drivers, there are many cases where conventional controls can be adapted to overcome driving difficulties. These adaptations can range from re-positioning one item—even the horn button or the dip switch—to fitting one of the proprietary systems of full adaptation which cater for leg or foot disabilities by giving hand control over accelerator, clutch and what would normally be the footbrake.

An arm or hand disability may be overcome by such fittings as a steering wheel device to which an artificial hand can be linked, leaving the good hand to do more work. Even a severe arm injury can sometimes be overcome by specialised equipment. In exceptional cases this can include special controls and even arrangements for the steering to be done by the driver's foot, although such things can be costly. Some disabilities which restrict the movement of the driver's body can be met by such relatively simple means as fitting extra mirrors, a specially padded seat or by lengthening the pedals. But others may be so severe that it has to be accepted that safe driving is impossible.

Do you fit your car?

This brings us back to fitting the car to the driver. Does your build affect your driving? If you are unusually tall the mirrors may need some re-arrangement to give you a full view, or you may need an extra one. If, on the other hand, you are very short, you may find some cars difficult to drive because of high facias or small pedals; or again you may need to re-position or add to the mirrors.

Your physical build may affect only certain driving operations; in this case you may need to do no more than adapt your driving method slightly to overcome the difficulty. In Chapter 10 we mention reversing as one of the times when your physique may affect your way of steering.

Good habits

Good habits are as much a part of safe driving as good technique. Most drivers have their own pet good habit which they recommend to other drivers. You may find yours among the following, or you may think some of them too obvious to mention. But they are all important—as habits—to good driving and to safety.

More haste, less speed

Even getting up early enough can be part of the story. If you don't start in time you may be tempted to hurry on the journey. Hurrying leads to mistakes, and mistakes can lead to accidents. Accidents mean arriving late—or even not at all. Leave in good time so that you don't have to rush.

Planning your journey

A map or road book will often show you the way round a town rather than through it. Give a little thought to rush hours and keep out of towns at difficult times.

Adapt your plan to weather conditions if possible. Mist or fog may mean a later start to a morning journey or an earlier start to an afternoon one to get you in before dark. Try to avoid driving in fog if you can, and so leave more room on the road for those who must be out in it.

If you like to run to a schedule on a long journey, plan it on the generous side. You will then probably find yourself running ahead of time instead of late and avoid any temptation to feel that you must catch up at all costs.

Regular daily journeys

If you drive to work every day, leave yourself more than the bare time for the journey, especially if you have no regular parking place and have to look for one. Don't be too thrusting or drive too fast just because you know the route well. Try to keep home and business worries out of your mind. They may creep back during traffic hold-ups, but switch them off before you move off again.

Your home ground

Don't let familiarity breed contempt. One day there *will* be something there.

Clothes

Comfortable clothes can make all the difference, especially on a long journey. Shoes are important too. Slippery soles are a menace on brake and clutch pedals. Shoes that are too wide can cause you to operate the accelerator by mistake at the same time as the brake pedal. For women, driving is certainly one of the occasions when shoe comfort is much more important than fashion. It is a sound idea to keep a pair of comfortable shoes—even if they are old ones—in the car.

Rest and refreshment

Don't go too long without a rest or try to press on if you are tired or in need of refreshment. (See also Chapter 14—Motorway driving.)

Health

Health affects driving; even a cold can put you below par. If you must drive when you are feeling under the weather, keep your speed down and give yourself more time to react.

Drugs and medicines

Always check with your doctor whether a medicine you may be taking will affect your ability to drive. And take his advice if he warns you against driving.

Drinking and driving

Apart from the penalties, these two things just do not mix.

Necessary stops

Don't be tempted to put off stops for natural functions. If you do, it will usually be at the expense of your concentration and safety.

Smoking

Smoking presents difficulties when you are driving. Lighting up, smoke, ash and so on all involve risks, even if you feel that smoking helps you to concentrate. If you really must smoke, remember the risks. Lighting a pipe certainly means a stop.

Radio

Listening to a car radio is a matter of taste and utility. Road bulletins, for example, can be very useful. But serious listening could affect your concentration.

Talking to passengers

Even at the risk of seeming rude, be ready to drop out of any conversation if the road needs more attention—or if an argument seems to be developing!

Clear windows

Like misted windows, stickers on the glass and dolls in the back window don't help anyone—except possibly as a warning to other drivers!

Seat belts

You are twice as safe wearing a seat belt as you are without one. Always wear your seat belt when you drive, and get your passengers to do so—even for the shortest journey. Safety apart, the steadying effect of a belt can help to prevent tiredness for both driver and passenger. Children should always ride in the back of the car, with a harness or belt, or in a safety seat, if possible.

Advance warning triangles

Get into the habit of carrying one of these red reflecting signs. Use it to warn other road users if your car becomes an obstruction as a result of a breakdown or accident. Stand the triangle on the road, usually in the same lane, well back from your car.

On a straight and level road the triangle should be at least 50 yards away from your car (although 100 yards is better). On a dual carriageway or motorway it should be 150 yards away *at least*. A warning triangle does not excuse your vehicle from stand-

At a busy junction like this one all works smoothly provided everyone does the right thing. Do you *always* stick to the rules?

ing in a dangerous position unnecessarily, and it is *not* a substitute for vehicle lights at night.

Where the road is not straight and level, be careful to put the triangle where an oncoming driver will see it *before* he comes to any bend or hump in the road. Where the road is so narrow or winding that the triangle might be run over, put it on the edge of the nearside verge or footpath.

Don't forget to take the sign with you when you can move your car.

All-round emergency flashers

Another way of warning other road users that you have stopped because of breakdown or accident is by means of a special switch that puts on all the direction indicators to flash together.

Soft ground

If you have to go on to soft ground to turn (or for any other manœuvre) don't let you *driving* wheels get on to it. Keep them on the road, or other hard surface, so that they don't dig in.

Litter

Don't throw anything out of your windows.

Acknowledging courtesies

It doesn't cost anything, and it makes things more pleasant, to acknowledge courtesy and help from other road users.

A last word

Finally, worthwhile experience takes time to acquire. Driving is no exception, and no one has ever 'seen it all'. You may be a new driver, recently freed of your instructor by having passed the test, or you may have had years on the road. Whatever stage you have reached as a driver, you will always be getting more experience from watching other people on the road. Judge the *quality* of what you see. Looking for and copying only the best of what you see will go a long way towards making (or keeping) you a good driver. It is easy, and perhaps natural, for drivers who took their test a long time ago—or who perhaps have never taken one—to be critical of less experienced drivers. But just how critical are you of *your own* driving? Do you always stick to the rules so that everyone knows what to expect?

New driver or old, the responsibility is yours; the road is no place for impatience, exhibitionism or selfishness. Your attitude to driving is as important as a detailed knowledge of the finer points of driving technique. This book has described, in some detail, the techniques necessary for good, safe driving. A proper attitude of mind is something that only *you* can develop. And here we come back full circle to Chapter 1 where we said that a good driver needs a sense of responsibility, concentration on the job of driving, patience and courtesy.

Summary

1

Automatic transmissions: what they do and how they help; getting the best out of them; the functions of the controls—drive, lock-up, kick-down, park—and how to use them; the importance of the handbrake; guarding against 'creep' and too fast tick-over; right-foot-only; using the accelerator gently; avoiding over-confidence

2

Semi-automatics: how they differ from automatics; pre-selectors

3

Overdrive: its value on long, fast journeys

4

Problems—and some solutions—for the disabled driver

5

Do you fit your car? How your build can affect your driving

6

Good habits: learning to acquire them yourself and recognise them in others. The right attitude to driving

The driving test

For most learner drivers, the driving test looms ahead as a major hurdle. It is also a general source of conversation whenever drivers are gathered together. There are probably more tall stories about the driving test than about any other motoring subject; the most remarkable thing about these stories is the number of times the old ones crop up again, years after they were first heard, in new and exaggerated forms. So although this book is directed to all drivers, it would not be out of place to describe, in this appendix, how the Department organises driving tests and exactly what the examiners are looking for.

There are about 400 centres, some of which are 'occasional'—that is, opened according to demand on one or more days each week, and staffed by examiners travelling from the permanent centres. There are about 1,100 driving examiners, all of whom have had to pass a very strict selection process, followed by at least six weeks' training. In the course of this training the Department makes sure that their driving is of a consistently high standard, and also that each examiner knows exactly the things he is expected to look for during a driving test.

Driving test centres are chosen with equal care. It would be nice to have centres and examiners to match the public demand town by town. But this is just not possible, because the centres have to be at places where there is enough parking space for candidates and where there are enough test routes which can be reached from the centres. Routes are carefully chosen to make sure that they are all roughly comparable—the same proportion of right and left turns, hills, pedestrian crossings and so on. The object of all this is to make sure, as far as possible, that all candidates in the driving test have to cope with the same sort of conditions whether they take the test in Inverness or Penzance.

The work that examiners do in actually carrying out tests is checked continuously by supervising examiners, who go out on driving tests and check the detailed records that examiners make of their tests. All this is to make as sure as possible that every candidate for the driving test has a proper and equal chance of showing the examiner, in the words of the Regulations, 'that he is competent to drive without danger to and with due consideration for other users of the road . . .'. This is *all* the examiner is concerned with. He is not concerned with whether the candidate is a man or a woman, old or young. Examiners do not have any quota of passes and failures, and there is certainly no truth in the story that 'they never pass anyone on Thursday afternoons'.

Now for the test itself. You can take the driving test at any one of the Department's centres. You send your application, with the fee, to the Traffic Area Office covering the centre at which you want to take the test. A few days later you will get an appointment card showing the date and time arranged for your test. If you cannot keep this appointment, let the Traffic Area Office know as soon as you can. If you cannot give three clear days' notice (not counting Saturdays, Sundays and Public Holidays), so that the appointment can be given to someone else, you will have to pay a fee for another appointment. Allow yourself plenty of time to get to the test centre. If you are late—for instance, because you had difficulty in parking—the examiner may not be able to take you. He has to keep to a timetable for the sake of the other candidates.

The first part of the test is easy. The examiner meets the candidate in the waiting room, where he gets his signature and sees his driving licence. On the way to the car he will ask whether the candidate is disabled in any way. Then he will carry out the eyesight test by asking the candidate to read a number plate. This will be at a distance well above the standard actually required. He will only come down to the exact distance (which will be measured with a tape, if necessary) if the candidate's eyesight is obviously borderline. Incidentally, every candidate should have checked for himself that his eyesight is up to the required standard. If it is not, he will have been committing an offence when driving anyway. The standard is to be able to read a number plate with the old $3\frac{1}{2}$-inch letters at a distance of 75 feet, or a plate with the newer, smaller symbols at 67 feet.

Next comes the actual driving part of the test. This will last about 30 minutes and falls into four parts:

1 Some straightforward driving to allow the candidate time to settle down and to help overcome 'test nerves'

2 A section leading up to the emergency stop

3 The manœuvres—reversing, turning and so on

4 Driving on busier roads

Before we discuss the actual requirements of the test in detail, here are two general points. First, the thing that candidates seem to notice most about the examiner is that he does not chat during the drive as an instructor would. The Department knows that some candidates would prefer the examiner to talk more. But others would not, and it is really better that candidates should be left alone to concentrate on the job of driving without having to worry about keeping up a conversation. So examiners keep their talking to the minimum necessary to let the candidate know what he is required to do—turn right, pull up and so on. Directions are given in plenty of time.

Second, the manœuvres. These are included as part of the driving test not because drivers will be doing them regularly in the course of everyday driving, but because they are very good exercises in control. For instance, turning in the road requires the use of all the controls—steering, accelerator, footbrake, handbrake and clutch—and the driver also has to keep a proper look-out at the same time.

Before driving off, remember your cockpit drill—doors, driving seat, mirror, seat belt, petrol. As the test proceeds, the examiner will make notes on his pad. Don't let this put you off. Concentrate on your job of driving, as the examiner will be concentrating on his. You start with a clean sheet, and although the examiner will be noting your mistakes he will disregard the minor ones in his final assessment. After all, few people can put up an absolutely faultless performance at anything when they have a critic sitting beside them. It is part of the examiner's job to decide whether mistakes are minor or serious in degree. A minor one does not result in a failure but a serious or dangerous one does.

The practical test

After you have both settled in your seats, the examiner will ask you to start up and drive away when you are ready. From then on, he will be marking your performance on his sheet, so it is useful to go through the points he will be looking for, as they are shown on the Statement of Failure given to unsuccessful candidates. All the driving techniques and procedures necessary to ensure success in the driving test have been described in this book. We shall refer back to them so that you can study them in detail and avoid failure points, or correct them if you collect a Statement of Failure after a test.

The first thing the examiner will want to see is that you—**Take suitable precautions before starting the engine.** This means, after the cockpit drill, making sure that the handbrake is on and the gear lever in neutral. (Study: Chapter 2—Handbrake; gear lever and gearbox; and Chapter 4—Starting the engine.)

Next, remember the drill for moving off as explained in Chapters 2, 3 and 4. You will be expected to do this smoothly, co-ordinating the handbrake, clutch and accelerator properly;

and to move off safely, without causing danger or inconvenience to anyone else on the road. This applies to every start you will have to make during the test, whether straight ahead, on the level, uphill, or moving out from behind a stationary vehicle. Any fault here will be marked under the heading—**Move off smoothly/ at an angle/on a gradient/on the level/straight ahead.** Remember too the other important thing about moving off safely —the look behind (Chapter 3). If you don't do this you will be faulted under the heading—**Look round before moving off.**

Throughout the test the examiner will be looking for reasonably smooth use of the controls. In other words, he will expect you to —**Make proper use of/accelerator/clutch/footbrake/gears/ handbrake/steering.** This means using the accelerator and clutch properly together to get a reasonably smooth start; using your footbrake firmly without being too harsh or sudden with it; being in the right gear according to the conditions and your road position; and changing gear in good time where you can see that it is going to be necessary—for instance, before going uphill or downhill, or before turning a corner. Incidentally, 'coasting' round a corner in neutral or with the clutch pedal held down is regarded as a serious fault because it reduces your control over the car. The proper use of these controls is so fundamental to good driving that a large part of this book has been devoted to it— there are many references in Chapters 2, 4, 5, 6, 9 and 10.

During the whole time you are driving the examiner will be building up a picture of your ability and common sense as a driver. There are five 'road behaviour' points which go towards making up this picture. The first is your general sense of position- ing for normal driving. The examiner will expect you to— **Keep well to the left in normal driving**—that is, except when you intend to turn right, overtake or pass parked vehicles or any other obstruction in the road. This does not mean driving along with your nearside wheels in the gutter. You need to choose a happy medium between this and being too far out towards the middle of the road. Where there are lane lines marked on the road, keep in the middle of your lane. You will find references to these points in Chapters 5, 9, 11 and 12.

Next, speed. Here again, the examiner will expect you to suit your speed to the road and traffic conditions. Crawling along unreasonably slowly on a clear road, perhaps holding up traffic behind you, would be regarded as a serious fault. You would be marked because you did not—**Make normal progress to suit varying road and traffic conditions.** Proper anticipation plays a large part in helping you to decide on the right speed, and it is just as important in avoiding the opposite fault of driving too fast. The examiner will expect you to obey the Highway Code rule about never driving so fast that you cannot stop well within the distance you can see to be clear; and to show him that you are ready to slow down (or keep your speed down) as necessary.

If you don't, or if you break the speed limit, you will be marked because you did not—**Exercise proper care in the use of speed.** You will find references to choosing the proper speed for general driving and when coming up to corners, bends, junctions and so on in Chapters 5, 6, 7, 8, 9, 11 and 12, together with another important point about speed—keeping a safe distance behind the vehicle in front.

The other two 'general behaviour' points also go together— mirror and signals. The mirror is so important that the whole of Chapter 3 is devoted to it. Almost everything that is said in that chapter can be summed up in the words used to describe faults under this heading—**Make proper use of the mirror well before/signalling/changing direction/overtaking/stopping.** The important words here are 'use', which means not just looking in the mirror but acting on what you see; and 'well before', which mean exactly what they say.

Signals need to be given in time for other road users to see what you are going to do before you do it and to react safely. The examiner will be looking to see that you not only give the correct signals but also give them in good time and, when you are using direction indicators, that you make sure they are cancelled when they have served their purpose. If you do not—**Give signals/ correctly/in good time/by direction indicators/by arm** you will be faulted.

A word here about giving signals by arm. Examiners do not expect, or want, hand flapping at every possible opportunity. But they do want to know that you know what arm signals mean and how they should be given. You may be asked to use arm signals for part of the test, but don't worry if you are not. The examiner will not make a special point of this if he has already seen you giving them. (Some disabled drivers may not be asked to give arm signals.) The thing to remember about arm signals is that only those shown in the Highway Code (and on pages 42 and 43 in this book) should be used, and that they should be given decisively and in good time.

All this is summed up in the safe routine, *mirror—signal— manœuvre*. You will find references to correct signalling in more detail in Chapters 5, 6 and 11.

The examiner will also be watching to see how you deal with other road users. Here again there is a group of five fault headings. All of them are related in one way or another to proper antici- pation—that is, realising what other people are doing, are going to do or might do, and doing the right thing yourself to allow for them. Chapters 5 and 12 show the importance of thinking ahead and being prepared to deal with any situation smoothly and unhurriedly; the examiner will therefore be looking to see that you —**Show alertness and anticipation of the actions of/ cyclists/pedestrians/drivers.**

Having recognised a particular situation, you then have to show that you can deal with it properly—choosing the right time and place for overtaking; judging the right moment to complete a right turn across traffic coming the other way, and so on. The keynote is never to do anything which would hinder or balk other drivers; hold back if you are in doubt. Chapters 5, 7, 11 and 12 contain much advice on how to—**Overtake/meet/cross the path of/other vehicles safely.**

Crossroads and road junctions come under this heading too. The examiner will be watching to see that you apply the safe routine, *mirror—signal—manœuvre*, and the junction routine, *position—speed—look*; that you are in the correct position before and after the junction and that your speed is suitable. There will be many junctions on the test route; you will have to show the examiner that you can recognise the sort of junction, how important it is, and how to deal with it. If you follow all the advice in Chapters 5, 6 and 7 you will be able to—**Act properly at crossroads/road junctions.**

Dealing properly with other road users means that you must —**Allow adequate clearance to/cyclists/pedestrians/stationary vehicles.** In other words, give them plenty of room. Chapter 12 shows how important it is to be ready for pedestrians who suddenly step off the pavement or into the road from between parked vehicles, and for drivers or passengers getting out of parked cars. There is the story (true this time) of the examiner who had to mark his report sheet 'shaved elephant'. Clearly that driver was not allowing other road users enough room!

Almost every test route includes one or more pedestrian crossings. The fault marking on the Statement of Failure is rather long—**Pedestrian crossings/approach at a proper speed/stop when necessary/avoid overtaking at or approaching/avoid dangerous signals to pedestrians**— but it says all there is to say about things to avoid. Chapters 5, 8 and 12 show the proper way to use anticipation so that you approach these crossings safely.

At the beginning of the test the examiner will have asked you to follow the road ahead. In following 'the road ahead' you will be expected to notice and act on all traffic signs and signals, as well as signals given by other drivers. Ignoring a STOP sign, going through traffic lights at red or into a one-way street the wrong way—anything of this sort means failure. Signals by policemen, traffic wardens or school crossing patrols must be obeyed. Information signs such as hill signs, bend signs, lane arrows all come under this heading. You will find several references throughout Chapters 5–9 and in Chapter 12 to signs and signals of this sort, which add up to requiring you to—**Take correct and prompt action on all signals by/traffic signs/ traffic controllers/take appropriate action on signals given by other road users.**

Now for the special exercises you will be asked to do during a driving test—not one after the other, but spaced out with normal driving in between. The first is the emergency stop.

Fairly early in the test, while you are pulled up at the kerb, the examiner will explain that he will give you a signal to stop the car as you would in an emergency such as a child running across the road. Then, when you are driving at a reasonable speed and he has made sure that an emergency stop would be safe, the examiner will give you the signal and expect to see you

—**Stop vehicle in emergency/promptly and under control.** Notice the two parts; promptly, which means reacting quickly and stopping as soon as you can; and under control, which means keeping your car in a straight line. If you lock the wheels you may go out of control and skid. You will find this particular subject of stopping in an emergency dealt with in Chapter 4, and Chapters 2, 5 and 13 also have useful information about the way brakes operate and how to use them properly.

The second exercise that you will be required to do is— **Reverse into a limited opening either to the right or left/ under control/with reasonable accuracy/with proper observation.** If you are driving a car you will be asked to reverse into a side road or other opening on the left. The examiner will ask you to stop on the left before the opening and will then tell you just what you have to do—drive past the opening, stop again in a position from which you can back in, and then drive in reverse round the corner, straighten up and go back for a reasonable distance.

As you pass the corner, look into the road or opening and weigh it up; stop reasonably close to the kerb, but not so close as to make it unnecessarily difficult for you to reverse. When you reverse, keep your engine speed down so that the car moves slowly and your steering is fully effective. Remember which way your front wheels are pointing. Keep reasonably close to the kerb as you go round the corner and after you have straightened up to drive back for some distance. You should certainly keep on your own side of the road. The other thing to remember about reversing is that you must keep a proper look-out all the time for other vehicles and pedestrians. Remember that the front of your car will swing out towards the middle of the road as you turn.

If you are driving a small van or other vehicle without a clear view to the rear, you may be asked to reverse into an opening on the right. This involves different positioning, but it is explained in detail in Chapter 10 under the heading of 'Reversing'.

The last exercise is to turn round in the road. The idea is to show the examiner that you can manœuvre your vehicle in a restricted space smoothly and safely. The important thing is to take your time, letting the car move as slowly as possible but turning the steering wheel as briskly as you can. This exercise is sometimes called the 'three-point turn', but this is a bit misleading because the examiner will not necessarily expect you to complete the turn in three movements. The number of backward and forward movements you need to make certainly depends partly on how neatly you use the controls. But it also depends on the size and steering of your car, as well as the width of the road. The examiner will make allowance for these things. Finally, as with any other manœuvre, you must keep a good look-out all the time. If other traffic comes along while you are turning, be ready to stop and let it pass. Studying these points, and the section of Chapter 10 which deals with turning in the road, will help you to—**Turn round by means of forward and reverse gears/under control/with reasonable accuracy/ with proper observation.**

We have mentioned several times that the examiner will ask you to stop at various places during the driving test. And there will also be the most welcome stop of all—the one at the end of your test. Whenever you stop, the examiner will expect you to choose a safe place and to pull up as close to the side of the road as you reasonably can. He will not try to trap you by asking you to pull up where stopping is illegal. Sometimes he will be fairly exact about where he wants you to stop—for instance, before he gives you the instructions about reversing into an opening. But otherwise, you should choose a place where *you* think you can safely stop long enough for the examiner to give you further directions. If you don't pick a suitable spot you may find yourself with a fault marked because you did not—**Select safe position(s) for normal stop(s).**

The oral test

We have now been through the headings under which driving faults are marked on an unsuccessful candidate's Statement of Failure. But there is still one more part of the test. After getting back to the centre at the end of the driving part of the test, the examiner will ask questions to test your knowledge of the Highway Code and other motoring matters such as skidding, the importance of correct tyre pressures, and other similar general points. When the test is so near its end, and you are naturally keyed up about the result, the examiner will not expect a 100-percent answer to every question he asks, nor want you to recite the Highway Code parrot fashion. What he will expect are common-sense answers which show that you know the Code and have a reasonable knowledge of your responsibilities as a driver.

After the test

As soon as he has finished asking you these questions, the examiner will tell you whether you have passed or failed. If you have passed he will give you the much-desired Certificate of Competence and ask you to sign it. You use this form to get your full driving licence.

If you have not passed, the examiner will mark your most serious driving faults on a Statement of Failure under the various headings we have talked about in this chapter. This form is almost as important as the Certificate of Competence—although a lot less welcome—because it shows both you and your instructor where you have gone wrong. At one time examiners used to explain verbally to unsuccessful candidates the reasons for their failure. But this just did not work. Sometimes candidates were so upset at not having passed that they could not take in what the examiner was saying; sometimes they misunderstood it; and sometimes they did not believe it. It is really much better in the long run, both for an unsuccessful candidate and for his instructor, to be able to sit down quietly afterwards, go through the various faults which have been marked and concentrate on putting them right.

But anyone who has really studied this book, paid attention to everything a good instructor has told him, and put it all into practice during the driving test should have no difficulty in qualifying for a 'pass'. The examiner will like it better too.

Conversion table of equivalent speeds

This table showing speed and distance in metric terms is included because of the increase in Continental travel.

Kilometres per hour	Metres per second	Miles per hour	Feet per second
5	1·4	3·1	4·6
10	2·8	6·2	9·1
15	4·2	9·3	13·7
20	5·6	12·4	18·2
25	6·9	15·5	22·8
30	8·3	18·6	27·3
35	9·7	21·7	31·9
40	11·1	24·8	36·5
45	12·5	27·9	41·0
50	13·9	31·0	45·6
55	15·3	34·1	50·1
60	16·7	37·3	54·7
65	18·0	40·4	59·2
70	19·4	43·5	63·8
75	20·8	46·6	68·4
80	22·2	49·7	72·9
85	23·6	52·8	77·5
90	25·0	55·9	82·0
95	26·4	59·0	86·6
100	27·8	62·1	91·1
105	29·2	65·2	95·7
110	30·6	68·3	100·2
115	31·9	71·5	104·8
120	33·3	74·6	109·4
125	34·7	77·7	114·0
130	36·1	80·8	118·5

One kilometre is almost exactly five-eighths of one mile

Index